COLORATURA ARIAS FOR
SOPRANO

Compiled and Edited by
Robert L. Larsen &
Martha Gerhart

Editorial Advisor: Richard Walters
Assistant Editor: Bryan Stanley

On the cover: "L'opéra de Paris" by Raoul Dufy
Used by permission of The Phillips Collection, Washington D.C.

ISBN 978-0-634-03208-0

www.schirmer.com
www.halleonard.com

G. SCHIRMER, *Inc.*

DISTRIBUTED BY

HAL•LEONARD®
CORPORATION
7777 W. BLUEMOUND RD. P.O. BOX 13819 MILWAUKEE, WI 53213

FOREWORD

The original soprano volume of the *G. Schirmer Opera Anthology* presented a rich selection of predominantly lyric arias. This subsequent additional collection in the series affords an exploration of coloratura and lyric coloratura repertoire in a spectrum of national and historical styles, from Handel to twentieth-century American opera. We are especially pleased to include several arias which appear for the first time in a modern, clean edition.

The titling of the book, *Coloratura Arias for Soprano*, rather than *Arias for Coloratura Soprano*, is deliberate. Though this music is florid and high, selected arias certainly can be appropriately and successfully negotiated by lyric voices.

Because of the nature of this repertoire and its performance traditions, optional cadenzas and other embellishments have been liberally included, in addition to presenting the original vocal line. We believe that not addressing important performance practices in this literature would be a disservice to the singer.

In the interest of maintaining a compact single volume, we have limited ourselves to one optional version of embellishment in nearly every situation, rather than presenting multiple choices. The suggestions in this edition are based on traditional interpretations and standard practices, augmented occasionally by practical insight. In the case of Handel's "Tornami a vagheggiar," stylistically appropriate *da capo* embellishments were not suggested, because, by nature, the possibilities are endless.

Principal sources for research were published cadenzas edited by Luigi Ricci and Estelle Liebling. Many other sources were also consulted, including landmark recorded performances by major artists. Singers should not hesitate to make their own investigations into further possibilities for cadenzas and *ossia* passages. We recommend that any choices be determined from research, taste, and an understanding of historically pertinent musical style.

As is common practice in aria editing, instances arose where cuts were made for a reasonable adaptation for solo voice and piano. Such issues are sometimes especially pronounced in the *bel canto* literature, where chorus and ensemble sections are typically omitted. We refer singers and pianists to the complete piano/vocal score of a particular opera to study any abbreviations made in this edition. Traditional cuts have been indicated within the complete and uncut music in a few arias.

We sincerely hope that this collection is both a musical inspiration and practical aid as you explore the endlessly fascinating operatic repertoire.

The Editors
June, 2002

CONTENTS

NOTES and TRANSLATIONS

The arias are presented chronologically by year of first performance.

ALCINA

1735
music by George Frideric Handel
libretto by Antonio Marchi (adapted from Fanzaglia's libretto *L'Isola di Alcina*, based on Ariosto's poem *Orlando Furioso*)

Tornami a vagheggiar

from Act I
setting: a magical island ruled by Alcina, a powerful sorceress
character: Morgana

Alcina's latest captive, Ruggiero, a brave knight, is magically spellbound by the sorceress' beauty and forgets about his betrothal to a certain Bradamante. Bradamante, in order to save her lover, hurries to the island disguised as her own brother, Ricciardo. Alcina's sister, Morgana, takes interest in this Ricciardo. Ruggiero, being led to believe that Ricciardo is vying for Alcina's love, desires that Ricciardo be punished.

At the conclusion of Act I Bradamante identifies herself to Ruggiero, but he only sees her as Ricciardo, a rival for Alcina. When he leaves, Morgana pleads with Bradamante to flee before Alcina changes her into a wild beast. Bradamante tells Morgana to find him and tell him that Ricciardo does not love Alcina, but another. When Morgana asks if it could be she, Bradamante assures her that it is. When Bradamante leaves, Morgana sings of her love for Ricciardo and her prayers that "he" will soon return.

"Tornami a vagheggiar" quickly became one of Handel's most famous arias, and it has in some productions been re-assigned to Alcina.

Tornami a vagheggiar,	*Come back to woo me;*
te solo vuol amar quest'anima fedel,	*only you does this faithful soul wish to love,*
caro mio bene, caro!	*my dearly beloved, dear one!*
Già ti donai il mio cor:	*I have already given you my heart:*
fido sarà'l mio amor;	*my love will be true;*
mai ti sarò crudel, cara mia spene.	*never will I be cruel to you, my dear hope.*

LES DEUX AVARES

(The Two Misers)
1770
music by André Grétry
libretto by C. G. Fenouillot de Falbaire

Plus de dépit, plus de tristesse

from Act I
setting: a square in Smyrna with houses, a pyramid, and a well
character: Henriette

Henriette is the niece of Gripon, a moneylender who has fled France for Turkey. She loves and is loved by Jérome, the nephew of the miser Martin who lives across the street from Gripon. The uncles are not fond of their young relatives because they may want to marry and claim inheritances. Henriette's nurse, Madelon, has just shown the young lovers some of Gripon's hidden treasures, but they are far more interested in the riches they find in each other.

Plus de dépit, plus de tristesse,	*No more spite, no more sadness*
dès que je puis voler vers toi.	*as soon as I can fly to you.*
De Gripon je plains la faiblesse,	*I am sorry for the failings of Gripon,*
et je chante quand je te vois.	*and I sing when I see you.*
Il se croit riche;	*He believes himself wealthy;*
ô le pauvre homme!	*oh, the poor man!*
L'or et l'argent sont tout son bien.	*Gold and silver are all his possessions.*
Moi, j'ai le cœur de Jérôme;	*As for me, I possess the heart of Jerome;*
mon trésor vaut mieux que le sien.	*my treasure is worth more than his.*

DIE ENTFÜHRUNG AUS DEM SERAIL
(The Abduction from the Seraglio)
1782
music by Wolfgang Amadeus Mozart
libretto by Gottlieb Stephanie the younger (after a libretto by Christoph Friedrich Bretzner)

Durch Zärtlichkeit und Schmeicheln

from Act II
Setting: the coast of Turkey, the 16th century; the Palace of the Pasha Selim
Character: Blonde

Konstanze, an English lady, and her maid, Blonde, have been carried off by Turkish pirates to the Palace of the Pasha Selim where the Pasha has respectfully but firmly declared his interest in Konstanze. Blonde finds herself having to fend off old Osmin, the overseer of the Pasha's harem. She does so with wit and charm, leaving him blustering at the foolhardiness of English men in allowing their women so much liberty.

Durch Zärtlichkeit und Schmeicheln,	*Through tenderness and flattery,*
Gefälligkeit und Scherzen	*kindness and fun,*
erobert man die Herzen	*one conquers the hearts*
der guten Mädchen leicht.	*of good-natured girls easily.*
Doch mürrisches Befehlen	*But surely domineering*
und Poltern, Zanken, Plagen	*and rumbling, wrangling, plaguing*
macht, daß in wenig Tagen	*make within a few days*
so Lieb' als Treu' entweicht.	*love, as well as loyalty, vanish.*

DER SCHAUSPIELDIREKTOR
(The Impresario)
1786
music by Wolfgang Amadeus Mozart
libretto by Gottlieb Stephanie the younger (paralleling librettos by Metastasio, Goldoni, Bertati, and Calzabigi)

Da schlägt die Abschiedsstunde

in one act
setting: the rehearsal rooms of an opera house
character: Madame Herz

An impresario is given the task of rescuing an opera company from dire circumstances. Among his problems is the difficulty of choosing between an aging diva and a young aspiring soubrette. In this aria the reigning soprano, with her prodigious talents and experience, attempts to stake out her territory.

Da schlägt die Abschiedsstunde,	*Now tolls the parting hour,*
um grausam uns zu trennen.	*to cruelly separate us.*
Wie werd' ich leben können,	*How shall I be able to live,*
o Damon, ohne dich?	*oh Damon, without you?*
Ich will dich begleiten,	*I wish to be with you*
im Geist dir zur Seiten	*in spirit, by your side,*
schweben um dich.	*to hover around you.*
Und du, vielleicht auf ewig	*And you perhaps forever*
vergißt dafür du mich! Doch nein!	*you will rather forget me. Surely not!*
Wie fällt mir so was ein?	*Why do I think such a thing?*
Du kannst gewiß nicht treulos sein,	*You can certainly not be untrue,*
ach nein.	*ah, no.*
Ein Herz, das so der Abschied kränket,	*A heart which parting hurts so much*
dem ist kein Wankelmut bekannt!	*does not know inconstancy!*
Wohin es auch das Schicksal lenket,	*Wheresoever destiny leads it,*
nichts trennt das festgeknüpfte Band.	*nothing severs the firmly united bond.*

DIE ZAUBERFLÖTE

(The Magic Flute)
1791
music by Wolfgang Amadeus Mozart
libretto by Emanuel Schikaneder (based on Liebeskind's *Lulu, oder Die Zauberflöte*, after a fairy tale by Wieland)

O zittre nicht, mein lieber Sohn

from Act I, scene 1
setting: Legendary; a wild rocky pass
character: Queen of the Night

The Queen of the Night appears from out of a cloud to Tamino, a prince lost in a strange land. She gives him a portrait of her daughter who has been stolen from her. She swears that the beautiful girl will be his once she is set free from her captors.

O zittre nicht, mein lieber Sohn;	*Oh tremble not, my dear son;*
du bist unschuldig, weise, fromm.	*you are guiltless, wise, pious.*
Ein Jüngling, so wie du, vermag am besten	*A young man such as you is best able*
das tiefbetrübte Mutterherz zu trösten.	*to console the deeply afflicted mother's heart.*
Zum Leiden bin ich auserkoren,	*For suffering am I destined,*
denn meine Tochter fehlet mir.	*as my daughter is absent from me.*
Durch sie ging all mein Glück verloren;	*Because of her all my happiness was lost;*
ein Bösewicht entfloh mit ihr.	*a villain took flight with her.*
Noch seh' ich ihr Zittern	*Still I see her trembling*
mit bangem Erschüttern,	*with fearful emotion,*
ihr ängstliches Beben,	*her anxious quivering,*
ihr schüchternes Streben.	*her meek struggle.*
Ich mußte sie mir rauben sehen.	*I had to watch her bereft of me.*
«Ach helft!» war alles was sie sprach	*"Ah, help!" was all that she said*
allein vergebens war ihr Flehen,	*but in vain was her supplication,*
denn meine Hilfe war zu schwach.	*for my help was too feeble.*
Du wirst sie zu befreien gehen;	*You will go to free her;*
du wirst der Tochter Retter sein, ja!	*you will be the daughter's rescuer yes!*
Und werd' ich dich als Sieger sehen,	*And when I see you as victor,*
so sei sie dann auf ewig dein!	*so may she then be forever yours!*

Der Hölle Rache

from Act II, scene 3
setting: Legendary; the garden in the palace of Sarastro, High Priest of the Temple of Isis
character: Queen of the Night

The Queen rescues her daughter, Pamina, from the clutches of Monostatos, a Moorish slave in the palace. The Queen then gives Pamina a dagger and orders her to kill Sarastro, the High Priest.

Der Hölle Rache kocht	*The rage of hell seethes*
in meinem Herzen,	*in my heart;*
Tod und Verzweiflung flammet	*death and despair flame*
um mich her!	*all around me!*
Fühlt nicht durch dich Sarastro	*If Sarastro does not feel, through you,*
Todesschmerzen,	*the pain of death,*
so bist du meine	*then you will be*
Tochter nimmermehr,	*my daughter nevermore*
nein, meine Tochter nimmermehr.	*no, my daughter nevermore.*
Verstoßen sei auf ewig,	*May you be rejected forever;*
verlassen sei auf ewig,	*may you be forsaken forever.*
zertrümmert sei'n auf ewig	*Shattered be forever*
alle Bande der Natur,	*all the bonds of nature*

wenn nicht durch dich	*if not, through you,*
Sarastro wird erblassen!	*Sarastro will die!*
Hört, Rachegötter!	*Hear, gods of vengeance!*
Hört der Mutter Schwur!	*Hear a mother's vow!*

IL BARBIERE DI SIVIGLIA
(The Barber of Seville)
1816
music by Gioachino Rossini
libretto by Cesare Sterbini (after *Le Barbier de Séville*, a comedy by Pierre Augustin Caron de Beaumarchais)

Una voce poco fa

from Act I, scene 2 (or Act II)
setting: Seville, Spain, the 17th century; a drawing room in the house of Don Bartolo
character: Rosina

A young man has been serenading 16-year-old Rosina, the ward of Don Bartolo. He introduced himself to her as a student, Lindoro, but he's actually Count Almaviva in disguise. She is sure she is in love and has written a letter to him for which she's anxious to find a messenger.

Though the libretto is set in the 17th century, productions of the opera are often set in the 18th century.

Una voce poco fa	*A voice, a little while ago,*
qui nel cor mi risuonò,	*echoed here in my heart;*
il mio cor ferito è già,	*my heart is wounded now,*
e Lindor fu che il piagò.	*and it was Lindoro who covered it with wounds.*
Sì, Lindoro mio sarà,	*Yes, Lindoro will be mine—*
lo giurai, la vincerò.	*I've sworn it, I shall win.*
Il tutor ricuserà,	*My guardian will object.*
io l'ingegno aguzzerò,	*I, quick-witted, will be sharp;*
alla fin s'accheterà,	*in the end he will acquiesce,*
e contenta io resterò.	*and I will be content.*
Io sono docile,	*I am submissive,*
son rispettosa,	*I'm respectful,*
sono ubbidiente,	*I'm obedient,*
dolce, amorosa;	*sweet, affectionate.*
mi lascio reggere,	*I allow myself to be governed;*
mi fò guidar.	*I let myself be guided.*
Ma se mi toccano	*But if they touch me*
dov'è il mio debole,	*where my sensitive spot is,*
sarò una vipera,	*I will be a viper,*
e cento trappole	*and I'll cause a hundred tricks*
prima di cedere farò giocar.	*to be played before giving in.*

LA SONNAMBULA
(The Sleepwalker)
1831
music by Vincenzo Bellini
libretto by Felice Romani (after *La Somnambule*, a ballet-pantomine by Eugène Scribe)

Care compagne...Come per me sereno

from Act I, scene 1
setting: a Swiss mountain village, the early 19th century; the village square outside an inn
character: Amina

Amina, an orphan girl adopted by the mill owner and his wife, Teresa, is about to be married to the wealthy peasant Elvino. The villagers sing the praises of the lovely young girl who responds with gratitude to them and to the mother she never knew who gave her life that she might know this joyful day.

8

Care compagne,	Dear companions,
e voi, teneri amici,	and you, kind friends
che alla gioia mia tanta parte prendete,	who share so much in my joy,
oh come dolci scendon d'Amina al core	oh, how sweetly fall upon the heart of Amina
i canti che v'inspira il vostro amore!	the songs which your love inspires in you!

A te, diletta, tenera madre,	To you, beloved gentle mother,
che a sì lieto giorno	who for this so happy day
me orfanella serbasti,	saved me, an orphan,
a te favelli questo, dal cor più	may speak these sweet tears,
che dal ciglio espresso,	of joy and this embrace
dolce pianto di gioia, e quest'amplesso.	expressed more from my heart than from my eyes.

Compagne…teneri amici…	Companions…kind friends…
Ah! madre…ah! qual gioia!	Oh, mother!…Oh, what joy!

Come per me sereno oggi rinacque il dì!	How peacefully for me is this day reborn!
Come il terren fiorì,	How the earth has flowered,
come fiorì	how it has blossomed
più bello e ameno!	more beautifully and agreeably!

Mai di più lieto aspetto	Never has nature glowed
natura non brillò;	with happier countenance;
amor la colorò, amor del mio diletto.	love has colored it—love of my dear one.

Sovra il sen la man mi posa;	Place your hand upon my breast;
palpitar, balzar lo senti:	feel it throb, beat:
egli è il cor che i suoi contenti	it is the heart which does not have the strength
non ha forza a sostener.	to sustain its happiness.
Ah, non ha forza a sostener,	Alas, it does not have the strength to sustain,
ah no.	ah, no.
Cari amici, amata madre!	Dear friends, beloved mother!

Ah! lo sento, è il mio core,	Ah, I feel it! It's my heart—
ah, sì, balzar lo sento, lo sento balzar!	ah yes, I feel it leap; I feel it leap!

Ah! non credea…Ah! non giunge

from Act II, scene 2
setting: a Swiss mountain village, the early 19th century; the village square, on the roof of a mill, night
character: Amina

Amina is a sleepwalker and is discovered in the room of the visiting nobleman, Rodolfo. Elvino, believing Amina faithless, is about to wed the innkeeper, Lisa, out of spite, when the distraught and heartbroken Amina is seen by the villagers precariously making her way, lantern in hand, over the roof of the mill. She sings a beautiful cavatina that likens the dead flowers that her beloved once gave her to the transience of love. Family and friends watch breathlessly in fear of her falling. Finally Elvino rushes to her and kneels at her feet. She wakes and, with a cry of delight, falls in her lover's arms. The opera concludes with her song of joy at being reunited with her beloved.

Ah! non credea mirarti	Ah, I did not think I would see you
sì presto estinto, o fiore;	so soon withered, oh flower;
passasti al par d'amore,	you faded just like love,
che un giorno sol durò.	which for one day only endured.
Potria novel vigore il pianto	My tears might be able to restore
mio recarti,	strength to you;
ma ravvivar l'amore il pianto mio,	but my weeping cannot revive love,
ah, no, non può!	ah, no!

Ah! non giunge uman pensiero	Ah, human thought cannot attain
al contento ond'io son piena:	the happiness with which I'm filled:
A' miei sensi io credo appena;	I can hardly believe my senses;
tu m'affida, o mio tesor!	trust me, oh my treasure!

Ah! mi abbraccia,
e sempre insieme,
sempre uniti in una speme,
della terra in cui viviamo
ci formiamo un ciel d'amor.
Ah!

Ah, embrace me;
and always together,
always united in one hope,
from the earth on which we dwell
we will create a heaven of love.
Ah!

LUCIA DI LAMMERMOOR
(Lucy of Lammermoor)
1835
music by Gaetano Donizetti
libretto by Salvatore Cammarano (after Sir Walter Scott's novel *The Bride of Lammermoor*)

Regnava nel silenzio

from Act I
setting: Scotland, the late 16th century; near a fountain in the park of the Lammermoor castle at evening
character: Lucia

Lucia (Lucy), the sister of Enrico (Lord Henry Ashton), was saved from the attack of a wild boar by Edgardo (Edgar) of Ravenswood, the mortal enemy of the Lammermoors. She now meets with Edgardo often and is waiting for him at this moment with her companion, Alice. She muses on the doleful legend of the fountain and then dispels her gloom with thoughts of her love for Edgardo.

Regnava nel silenzio
   alta la notte e bruna...
colpia la fonte un pallido
   raggio di tetra luna...
quando un sommesso gemito
fra l'aure udir si fè
ed ecco, ecco su quel margine
l'ombra mostrarsi a me, ah!

The night was reigning in the silence
   deep and dark...
a pale ray of gloomy moonlight
   was striking the fountain...
when a soft moan
through the air made itself heard
and suddenly here, here on that fountain's edge
the ghost appeared to me—ah!

Qual di chi parla,
muoversi il labbro suo vedea,
e con la mano esanime
chiamarmi a sé parea;
stette un momento immobile,
poi ratta dileguò,
e l'onda pria sì limpida
di sangue rosseggiò,
sì, pria sì limpida,
ahi! rosseggiò.

Like one who is speaking,
I saw her move her lips,
and, with bloodless hand,
she seemed to beckon me to her;
she stayed for a moment immobile,
then swiftly vanished,
and the water, before so clear,
reddened with blood—
yes, so clear before,
alas, turned red!

Egli è luce a giorni miei,
è conforto al mio penar.

He is light to my days,
is comfort to my suffering.

Quando rapito in estasi
del più cocente ardore,
col favellar del core
mi giura eterna fè,
gli affanni miei dimentico;
gioia diviene il pianto.
Parmi che a lui d'accanto
si schiuda il ciel per me.
Ah!

When, carried away in ecstasy
of the most burning ardor,
with heartfelt words
he swears to me eternal faithfulness,
I forget my sorrows;
weeping turns to joy.
It seems to me that, at his side,
heaven opens up for me.
Ah!

A lui d'accanto
si schiuda il ciel per me, ah!
Sì, a lui d'accanto
par si schiuda il ciel per me.

At his side
heaven opens up for me, ah!
Yes, at his side
heaven seems to open up for me.

Il dolce suono…Spargi d'amaro pianto
(Mad Scene)

from Act II
setting: Scotland, the late 16th century; the great hall of Lammermoor castle, evening
character: Lucia

Raimondo (Raymond), Lucia's tutor, has just told an assemblage of wedding guests that he heard a groan in the bridal suite which he entered to find Lucia standing with knife in hand over the body of her dead husband, Arturo (Arthur) Bucklaw. Lucia suddenly enters, disheveled, in her white sleeping robes now stained with blood. She is pale as death and unconscious of her surroundings. She thinks she is with her beloved Edgardo by the fountain in the park where for a moment they are separated by the spirit in the fountain, but then they fly to a celestial altar where she is united with her rightful bridegroom at last.

Il dolce suono mi colpì di sua voce.	*The sweet tone of his voice struck me.*
Ah, quella voce m'è qui nel cor discesa.	*Ah, that voice settled here in my heart.*
Edgardo, io ti son resa,	*Edgardo, I am restored to you,*
Edgardo, ah, Edgardo mio, sì, ti son resa:	*Edgardo, ah my Edgardo, yes, I am restored to you:*
fuggita io son da tuoi nemici.	*I have escaped from your enemies.*
Un gelo mi serpeggia nel sen!	*A chill spreads through my breast!*
Trema ogni fibra, vacilla il piè!	*My every fiber trembles, my steps are unsteady!*
Presso la fonte meco t'assidi alquanto,	*By the fountain sit with me for a while—*
sì, presso la fonte meco t'assidi!	*yes, by the fountain sit with me!*
Ohimè! sorge il tremendo fantasma	*Alas! the horrible ghost looms up*
e ne separa!	*and separates us!*
Edgardo! ah! Il fantasma ne separa!	*Edgardo, ah, the ghost separates us!*
Qui ricovriamo, Edgardo,	*Here let us take shelter, Edgardo,*
a piè dell'ara.	*at the foot of the altar.*
Sparsa è di rose!	*It is strewn with roses!*
Un'armonia celeste, di', non ascolti?	*A heavenly harmony—tell me, do you not hear it?*
Ah! l'inno suona di nozze!	*Ah, the wedding hymn is sounding!*
Ah! l'inno di nozze!	*Ah, the wedding hymn!*
Il rito per noi s'appresta!	*The ceremony is being prepared for us!*
Oh me felice! Edgardo!	*Oh happy me! Edgardo!*
Oh gioia che si sente e non si dice!	*Oh, joy felt and not spoken!*
Ardon gl'incensi,	*The incense is burning,*
splendon le sacre faci,	*the sacred torches are shining;*
splendon intorno.	*they are shining all around.*
Ecco il ministro! porgimi la destra!	*Here is the minister! Offer me your right hand!*
Oh lieto giorno!	*Oh happy day!*
Alfin son tua, alfin sei mio,	*At last I am yours, at last you are mine;*
a me ti dona un Dio.	*God gives me to you.*
Ogni piacer più grato, sì,	*Every most welcomed pleasure of mine, yes,*
mi fia con te diviso, con te!	*will be shared with you, with you!*
Del ciel clemente un riso	*Life for us will be*
la vita a noi sarà!	*a happiness from merciful heaven.*
Spargi d'amaro pianto	*Sprinkle my earthly veil*
il mio terrestre velo,	*with bitter weeping,*
mentre lassù nel cielo io pregherò per te.	*while in heaven above I will pray for you.*
Al giunger tuo soltanto	*Only in joining you*
fia bello il ciel per me! ah sì, per me.	*will heaven be beautiful for me, ah yes, for me.*
Ah!	*Ah!*

I PURITANI

I Puritani di Scozia
(The Puritans of Scotland)
1835
music by Vincenzo Bellini
libretto by Count Carlo Pepoli (after *Têtes Rondes et Cavaliers*, a play by Jacques-Arsène Ancelot and Joseph Xavier Boniface *dit* Saintine)

O rendetemi la speme…Qui la voce

from Act II, the Mad Scene
setting: England, near Plymouth, during the Civil War between the supporters of Cromwell and the Stuarts
character: Elvira

Lord Walton, the Puritan Governor-General, has consented to allow his daughter Elvira to be married to the man she loves, Lord Arthur Talbot (Arturo), even though he is a royalist. But on the day of the planned nuptials Arturo learns that the widow of Charles I is in the castle under sentence of death. He is able to escape with the queen disguised in the wedding veil he had brought for Elvira. When the escape is discovered, Elvira, thinking herself deserted, loses her reason. In the next scene in the Puritan encampment Elvira wanders in, utterly distracted, reflecting on the wedding that never took place.

O rendetemi la speme	*Either give me back hope*
o lasciatemi morir.	*or let me die.*
Qui la voce sua soave	*Here his gentle voice*
mi chiamava... e poi sparì.	*called to me, and then vanished.*
Qui giurava esser fedele;	*Here he swore to be faithful;*
qui il giurava, e poi,	*here he swore it, and then*
crudele, ei mi fuggì!	*cruel man he fled from me!*
Ah! mai più qui assorti insieme	*Ah, nevermore rapt here together*
nella gioia dei sospir.	*in the joy of yearning!*
Ah! rendetemi la speme,	*Ah, give me back hope,*
o lasciatemi morir.	*or let me die!*
Vien, diletto, è in ciel la luna!	*Come, beloved, the moon is in the sky!*
Tutto tace intorno intorno;	*All is silent roundabout;*
finchè spunti in cielo il giorno,	*until day breaks in the sky,*
vien, ti posa sul mio cor!	*come, rest upon my heart!*
Deh! t'affretta, o Arturo mio;	*Please hasten, oh my Arthur;*
riedi, o caro, alla tua Elvira:	*return, oh dear one, to your Elvira:*
essa piange e ti sospira.	*she weeps and yearns for you.*
Vien, o caro, all'amore,	*Come, oh dear one, to love;*
ah vieni, vien all'amor.	*Ah, come, come to love.*
Riedi all'amore,	*Return to love;*
ah riedi all'amor.	*ah, return to love.*
Ah riedi al primo amor!	*Ah, return to your first love!*

LINDA DI CHAMOUNIX

1842
music by Gaetano Donizetti
libretto by Gaetano Rossi (after *La Grâce de Dieu* by Gustave Lemoine and Adolphe-Philippe d'Ennery)

Ah, tardai troppo…O luce di quest'anima

from Act I
setting: Chamounix, a village of Sarny, France, and Paris, 1760, during the reign of Loius XV; just after dawn in the village
character: Linda

Linda, a farmer's daughter, enters. She was to have met with her lover, Carlo, a penniless painter (who is later revealed to be the wealthy Vicomte de Sirval), but was late for the rendezvous and only found the flowers that he left for her. She is clearly in love and determines to see her beau again very soon.

Ah, tardai troppo,
e al nostro favorito convegno
io non trovai il mio diletto Carlo.
E chi sa mai quant'egli avrà sofferto,
ma non al par di me!

Pegno d'amore questi fior mi lasciò!
Tenero core! E per quel core io l'amo,
unico di lui bene.
Poveri entrambi siamo;
viviam d'amor, di speme.
Pittore ignoto ancora,
egli s'innalzerà co' suoi talenti!
Sarò sua sposa allora…
Oh noi contenti!

O luce di quest'anima, delizia, amore e vita,
la nostra sorte unita in terra, in ciel sarà.
Deh vieni a me,
riposati su questo cor che t'ama,
che te sospira e brama,
che per te sol vivrà…

O luce di quest'anima,
amor, delizia e vita,
unita nostra sorte in terra, in ciel sarà.
Vieni…Ah!

Vieni al mio core che te sospira,
che per te solo, sì, sol vivrà per te.

Ah, I delayed too long;
and at our favorite meeting place
I did not find my dearly beloved Carlo.
Who knows how much he will have suffered—
but not as much as I!

As a pledge of love he left me these flowers!
Tender heart! And I love him for that heart,
his unique treasure.
Impoverished are we both;
we live on love, on hope.
A painter yet unrecognized,
he will advance because of his talents!
I will be his wife then…
Oh happy we!

Oh light of this soul, delight, love, and life,
our destiny will be united on earth, in heaven.
Please come to me;
rest upon this heart which loves you,
which sighs and yearns for you,
which for you alone will live…

Oh light of this soul,
love, delight, and life,
united will be our destiny on earth, in heaven.
Come...Ah!

Come to my heart which yearns for you,
which for you alone, yes, will live only for you.

LA FILLE DU RÉGIMENT
(The Daughter of the Regiment)
1840
music by Gaetano Donizetti
libretto by Jules-Henri Vernoy de Saint-Georges and Jean-François-Alfred Bayard

Chacun le sait

from Act I
setting: in the mountains of the Swiss Tyrol, 1815
character: Marie

Marie was found on a battlefield when she was just a baby and brought up by the entire Twenty-first Regiment of Grenadiers. When a stranger is dragged in having been discovered prowling around the camp Marie exclaims that he is the fellow who saved her life when she almost plunged over a precipice. His name is Tonio, and he decides to become a soldier so that he can remain near Marie. The regiment toasts the new recruit and calls upon Marie to sing the "Song of the Regiment."

Ah!
Chacun le sait, chacun le dit:
le régiment par excellence,
le seul à qui l'on fass' crédit
dans tous les cabarets de France.
Le régiment: en tous pays
l'effroi des amants, des maris,
mais de la beauté bien suprême!

Il est là, morbleu!
Le voilà, corbleu!
Il est là, le voilà,
le beau vingt et unième!

Ah!
Everybody knows it, everybody says it:
the regiment "par excellence,"
the only one that people trust
in all the pubs of France.
The regiment: in all countries
the dread of lovers, of husbands,
but in handsomeness quite supreme!

Here it is, by God!
There it is, by Jove!
Here it is, there it is:
the handsome twenty-first!

Il a gagné tant de combats	*It has won so many battles*
que notre empereur, on le pense,	*that our emperor, we think,*
fera chacun de ses soldats,	*will make each of its soldiers,*
à la paix, maréchal de France!	*when peace comes, a marshal of France!*
Car c'est connu	*For it is known as*
le régiment le plus vainqueur,	*the regiment the most victorious,*
le plus charmant, qu'un sexe craint,	*the most attractive, which one sex fears*
et que l'autre aime.	*and the other loves.*
Vive le vingt et unième!	*Long live the twenty-first!*

DON PASQUALE

1843
music by Gaetano Donizetti
libretto by the composer and Giovanni Ruffini (after Angeli Anelli's libretto for Pavesi's *Ser Marcantonio*)

Quel guardo il cavaliere…So anch'io la virtù magica

from Act I, scene 2
setting: Rome in the early 19th century; Norina's apartment
character: Norina

Norina, a young widow who is in love with Ernesto, the nephew of old Don Pasquale, is reading a sentimental novel as the curtain rises. She tosses it aside to reveal her flirtatious and sprightly nature to the audience.

Quel guardo il cavaliere	*That glance pierced the knight*
in mezzo al cor trafisse;	*to the depths of his heart;*
piegò il ginocchio e disse:	*he fell on bended knee and said:*
Son vostro cavalier.	*I am your knight.*
E tanto era in quel guardo	*And there was in that glance such a*
sapor di paradiso	*taste of paradise*
che il cavalier Riccardo,	*that the knight Richard,*
tutto d'amor conquiso,	*totally conquered by love,*
giurò che ad altra mai	*swore that to another woman never*
non volgeria il pensier.	*would he turn his thoughts.*
Ah ah! Ah ah!	*Ha ha! Ha ha!*
So anch'io la virtù magica	*I too know the magic power*
d'un guardo a tempo e loco;	*of a glance at the right time and place;*
so anch'io come si bruciano	*I too know how hearts can smoulder*
i cori a lento foco.	*at a slow burn.*
D'un breve sorrisetto	*Of a fleeting little smile*
conosco anch'io l'effetto,	*I also know the effect,*
di menzognera lagrima,	*of a furtive tear,*
d'un subito languor.	*of a sudden languor.*
Conosco i mille modi	*I know the thousand ways*
dell'amorose frodi,	*of amorous tricks,*
i vezzi e l'arti facili	*the charms and easy skills*
per adescare un cor.	*for enticing a heart.*
So anch'io la virtù magica	*I too know the magic power*
per inspirare amor;	*for inspiring love;*
conosco l'effetto, ah sì,	*I know the effect, ah yes,*
per inspirare amor.	*of inspiring love.*
Ho testa bizzarra,	*I have an eccentric mind,*
son pronta, vivace,	*I'm quick-witted, high-spirited;*
brillare mi piace,	*I like to sparkle,*
mi piace scherzar.	*I like to have fun.*
Se monto in furore,	*If I fly into a rage,*
di rado sto al segno,	*rarely do I hit the target;*
ma in riso lo sdegno	*rather, I make the anger*
fo presto a cangiar.	*quickly change to laughter.*

Ho testa bizzarra,	*I have an eccentric mind,*
ma core eccellente. Ah!	*but an excellent heart. Ah!*
Ho testa bizzarra,	*I have an eccentric mind;*
son pronta e vivace.	*I'm quick-witted and high-spirited.*
Ah, mi piace scherzar.	*Ah, I like to have fun.*
Ho testa vivace,	*I have a lively mind;*
mi piace scherzar.	*I like to have fun.*
Ah, mi piace scherzar!	*Ah, I like to have fun!*

MARTHA

1847
music by Friedrich von Flotow
libretto by W. Friedrich [Friedrich Wilhelm Riese] (after a ballet-pantomime, *Lady Henriette, ou La Servante de Greenwich* by St. Georges)

Den Teuren zu versöhnen

from Act IV
setting: a farm near Richmond, England, during the reign of Queen Anne, c. 1710
character: Lady Harriet (Martha)

Lady Harriet Durham, Maid of Honour to Queen Anne, bored with life at court, ran off on holiday with Nancy, her maid in waiting. They played at being country girls (Lady Harriet called herself 'Martha') and managed to ensnare the hearts of two farmers. Now the farmers have learned the truth, and Lady Harriet's young man has plunged into a despondency verging on madness. In this aria she confesses her sincere love for him and vows to transform his despair into joy.

Zum treuen Freunde geh',	*Go to the faithful friend*
den Plan ihm zu entdecken,	*to reveal to him the plan*
den mein bereuend Herz	*which my repentant heart*
voll Zuversicht erdacht,	*has in full confidence devised,*
aus dumpfer Schwermut Traum	*from the melancholy dream*
den Teuren zu erwecken	*to arouse the dear man*
mit neuem Hoffnungsstrahl	*with a new ray of hope*
nach trüber Kerkernacht.	*after the gloomy prison night.*
Noch vernahm er nicht die Kunde,	*He has not yet learned the news,*
wie die Zukunft schön ihm tagt.	*how the future dawns fair upon him.*
Ja, ich heile selbst die Wunde,	*Yes, I myself will heal the hurt*
die ich schlug! Es sei gewagt,	*which I inflicted! Let it be risked,*
ja, ja, es sei gewagt!	*yes, yes, let it be risked!*
Den Teuren zu versöhnen	*To be reconciled with the dear man*
durch wahre Reu',	*through true repentance,*
sein Dasein zu verschönen	*to brighten his existence*
mit Lieb' und Treu',	*with love and devotion,*
mein Los mit ihm zu teilen,	*to share my destiny with him,*
durch's Leben hin zu eilen,	*to hasten through life with him*
ach, welch Glück!	*ah, what happiness!*
Ja, nun darf ich frei ihm sagen,	*Yes, now may I freely tell him*
wie mein Herz, seit ich ihn sah,	*how my heart, since I saw him,*
nur für ihn geschlagen!	*has been beating for him alone!*
Ja, wie sein Bild mir immer nah!	*Yes, how his image is always close to me!*
Ah! O seliger Gedanke,	*Ah! Oh blessed thought,*
o Hoffnungsschein!	*oh gleam of hope!*
Es sank die Trennungsschranke.	*The barriers of separation have given way.*
Mein wird er, ja, mein!	*He will be mine yes, mine!*
Ah!	*Ah!*

MANON LESCAUT
1856
music by Daniel François Auber
libretto by Eugène Scribe (after the novel by Antoine-François Prévost)

C'est l'histoire amoureuse
(Laughing Song)

from Act I
setting: Paris, the 18th century; Bacelin's restaurant and dancing house on the Boulevard du Temple

The young Manon and her lover Des Grieux have run up a large bill at Bacelin's. Manon has unfortunately given their purse to her cousin Lescaut who confesses when he joins them that he has gambled it away. The men sally forth to borrow a sum in the neighborhood leaving Manon hostage. She borrows a guitar ands sings a good-humored song about unrequited love. The tale amuses its teller and she bursts into laughter after almost every sentence. She is showered with gold and the attentions of the wealthy Marquis d'Hérigny.

This aria was often sung by Adelina Patti and Amelita Galli-Curci in the letter scene from Rossini's *Il Barbiere di Siviglia*.

M'y voici!	*Here, I've got it!*
Un instant, prête-moi	*Just a moment, will you lend me*
cette vieille guitare?	*that old guitar?*
La la la la la la la. Ah!	*La la la la la la. Ah!*
Pour peu que la chanson vous plaise,	*If only the song should please you,*
écoutez, grands et petits,	*listen, grown-ups and children, to*
la nouvelle Bourbonnaise	*the new bourbonnaise song*
dont s'amuse tout Paris! Ah!	*by which all Paris is being amused! Ah!*
C'est l'histoire amoureuse,	*This is the love story,*
autant que fabuleuse,	*however incredible,*
d'un galant fier à bras,	*of a gallant swaggerer,*
ah ah ah ah ah ah ah ah ah...	*ha, ha, ha, ha, ha, ha, ha, ha...*
d'un tendre commissaire	*of a tender-hearted commissioner*
que l'on croyait sévère	*whom people believed severe,*
et qui ne l'était pas!	*and who was not!*
Ah ah ah ah ah ah ah ah.	*Ha ha ha ha ha ha ha ha.*
Il aimait une belle, ah ah!	*He loved a beautiful woman, ha ha!*
Il en voulait, mais elle, ah ah,	*He desired her, but she, ha, ha,*
de lui ne voulait pas!	*did not desire him!*
Ah ah ah ah ah ah ah ah.	*Ha ha ha ha ha ha ha ha.*
Or, voulez-vous apprendre	*Well now, do you want to learn*
le nom de ce Léandre,	*the name of this Leander,*
traître comme Judas!	*traitorous as Judas?*
Son nom? Vous allez rire.	*His name? You're going to laugh.*
Je m'en vais vous le dire	*I'll tell it to you*
bien bas...tout bas...	*quite softly...very softly...*
Non, non, je ne le dirai pas!	*No, no, I will not tell it to you!*
La la la la la la la la...	*La la la la la la la...*
On le disait habile,	*People said he was clever,*
car dans la grande ville	*for in the city*
il est des magistrats!	*he is one of the judges on the bench!*
Ah ah ah ah ah ah ah ha.	*Ha ha ha ha ha ha ha.*
Il est des réverbères	*There are streetlamps*
vantés pour leurs lumières	*praised for their light*
et qui n'éclairent pas!	*and which do not illuminate!*
Ah ah ah ah ah ah ah ah.	*Ha ha ha ha ha ha ha ha.*
Au logis de la belle, ah ah,	*To the lodgings of the beauty, ha, ha,*
un soir que sans chandelle, ah ah,	*one evening when, without a candle, ha, ha,*
il veut porter ses pas,	*he meant to make his way,*
ah ah ah ah ah ah ah ah ah,	*ha ha ha ha ha ha ha ha,*
l'escalier était sombre,	*the stairway was dark,*
et sur son nez, dans l'ombre,	*and, on his nose, in the darkness,*
il tombe! Patatras!	*he fell! Crash!*

16

Ô galant commissaire,	Oh gallant commissioner,
alors que vers Cythère	when toward Cythera
vous porterez vos pas,	you proceed,
ah ah ah ah ah ah ah ah,	ha ha ha ha ha ha ha ha,
Diogène moderne,	you modern Diogenes,
prenez votre lanterne,	take your lantern,
de crainte de faux pas!	for fear of a stumble!
Ah ah ah ah ah ah ah ah.	Ha ha ha ha ha ha ha ha.
Mais c'est qu'à la lumière, ah ah,	But the fact is that in the light, ha, ha,
vous aurez peine à plaire, ah ah!	you will hardly be pleasing, ha ha!
Et dès qu'on vous verra,	And as soon as one sees you,
ah ah ah ah ah ah ah ah,	ha ha ha ha ha ha ha ha,
oui, rien qu'à votre face,	yes, at the mere sight of your face,
en faisant la grimace,	grimacing,
l'amour s'envolera.	love will fly away.
Pour calmer son délire,	In order to quiet his frenzy,
son nom je vais le dire	his name I'm going to tell you
bien bas...tout bas...	quite softly...very softly...
Non, non, je ne le dirai pas!	No, no, I will not tell it to you!
La la la la la la la la.	La la la la la la la la.

DINORAH
ou Le Pardon de Ploërmel
(Dinorah, or the Pardon of Ploërmel)
1859
music by Giacomo Meyerbeer
libretto by Jules Barbier and Michel Carré

Ombre légère
(Shadow Song)

from Act II
setting: Brittany, the 19th century; the village of Ploërmel and the countryside around it
character: Dinorah

On the day Dinorah was to be married to the goatherd Hoël, her father's house was destroyed by a storm. Her fiancé vowed to rebuild it and raced off to seek a treasure of which he had heard. Dinorah, believing to be deserted, wanders through the countryside seeking her lost beloved. In the beginning of Act II she enters the stage in moonlight and, seeing her shadow, imagines it to be a friend and dances for and with it.

La nuit est froide et sombre.	The night is cold and gloomy.
Ah! quel ennui d'errer seule	Ah, what tedium to wander alone
dans l'ombre!	in the darkness!
O joie! Enfin le ciel s'éclaire!	Oh joy! At last the sky brightens!
Je te retrouve, amie ingrate et chère!	I find you again, ungrateful and dear friend!
Bonjour! Tu veux savoir, je gage,	Good-day! You want to know, I wager,
quelles chansons d'amour,	which songs of love,
en te mêlant aux danses du village,	in mingling with the village dances,
tu chanteras à notre mariage?	you will sing at our marriage?
Allons, vite, prends ta leçon!	Come, quickly, take your lesson!
Hâte-toi d'apprendre danse et chanson!	Hurry up to learn dance and song!
Ombre légère, qui suis mes pas,	Fickle shadow, who follows my steps,
ne t'en va pas, non!	do not go away, no!
Fée ou chimère, qui m'est si chère,	Fay or fancy, who to me is so dear,
ne t'en va pas! Non, non, non!	do not go away! No, no, no!
Courons ensemble,	Let us run along in each other's company;
j'ai peur, je tremble	I am afraid, I tremble
quand tu t'en vas loin de moi!	when you go far away from me!
Ah! Ne t'en va pas!	Ah, do not go away!
À chaque aurore je te ravois!	At each daybreak I recover you!
Ah, reste encore;	Ah, stay longer;

danse à ma voix!	*dance to my voice!*
Pour te séduire je viens sourire;	*In order to lure you I will smile;*
je veux chanter!	*I want to sing!*
Approche-toi!	*Draw near!*
Viens, réponds-moi!	*Come, answer me!*
Chante avec moi!	*Sing with me!*
Ah! réponds!	*Ah, answer!*
Ah! c'est bien!	*Ah, that's good!*
Sais-tu bien qu'Hoël m'aime,	*Don't you know that Hoël loves me,*
et qu'aujourd'hui même	*and that this very day*
Dieu va pour toujours bénir nos amours?	*God is going to bless our love forever?*
Le sais-tu?	*Do you know it?*
Mais tu prends la fuite!	*But you are taking flight!*
Pourquoi me quitter, quand ma voix t'invite?	*Why leave me, when my voice invites you?*
La nuit m'environne!	*The night encompasses me!*
Je suis seule, hélas!	*I am alone, alas!*
Ah! reviens, sois bonne!	*Ah, come back; be good!*
Ah! c'est elle!	*Ah, it's she!*
Méchante, est-ce moi que l'on fuit?	*Cruel one, is it I who is shunned?*
Ombre légère…	*Fickle shadow…*
La, la, la…	*La, la, la…*
Ah! reste avec moi!	*Ah, stay with me!*

UN BALLO IN MASCHERA

(A Masked Ball)
1859
music by Giuseppe Verdi
libretto by Antonio Somma (after Eugène Scribe's libretto for Daniel-François Auber's *Gustavus III, ou Le Bal Masqué*)

Volta la terrea

from Act I
setting: the court at Stockholm, 1792 (or Boston, depending on the version played)
character: Oscar

In his audience chamber, a judge tells the King about a foreign woman whose lair is a haven for outlaws and criminals of sorts. The judge is anxious to have her exiled, but Oscar, a page and a great favorite of the King's, defends her, insisting that she is a great and wise soothsayer.

Volta la terrea fronte alle stelle	*With wan brow turned toward the stars,*
come sfavilla la sua pupilla,	*how her eye gleams*
quando alle belle	*when, to the beautiful women,*
il fin predice	*she predicts the end,*
mesto o felice dei loro amor!	*sad or happy, of their love!*
È con Lucifero d'accordo ognor,	*She is, with Lucifer, always in agreement*
Ah, sì!	*Ah, yes!*
Chi la profetica sua gonna afferra,	*Whoever grasps her prophetical skirt,*
o passi'l mare, voli alla guerra,	*whether he cross the sea or flee to war,*
le sue vicende soavi, amare	*his fortunes, sweet or bitter,*
da questa apprende	*from this woman will learn*
nel dubbio cor!	*in his doubting heart!*

MIGNON

1866
music by Ambroise Thomas
libretto by Jules Barbier and Michel Carré (after Goethe's novel *Wilhelm Meister's Lehrjahre*)

Je suis Titania

from Act II, scene 2
setting: the garden of the Tieffenbach Castle in Germany, the late 18th century
character: Philine

The actress has been performing in Shakespeare's *A Midsummer Night's Dream* in the castle. When it ends, she comes into the garden still costumed as queen of the fairies, attended by members of the audience and Wilhelm Meister, a student in whom she has shown great interest. All proclaim her beauty and talent and, in the flush of her triumph, she rewards them with a brilliant French polonaise or polacca.

Oui, pour ce soir	*Yes, for this evening*
je suis reine des fées!	*I am queen of the fairies!*
Voici mon sceptre d'or,	*Here is my sceptre of gold,*
et voici mes trophées!	*and here are my trophies!*
Je suis Titania la blonde.	*I am Titania the fair.*
Je suis Titania, fille de l'air!	*I am Titania, daughter of the air!*
En riant, je parcours le monde	*Laughing, I traverse the world*
plus vive que l'oiseau,	*more lively than the bird,*
plus prompte que l'éclair!	*more quick than the flash of lightning!*
Ah! Je parcours le monde!	*Ah! I traverse the world!*
La troupe folle des lutins	*The impish band of sprites*
suit mon char qui vole	*follows my chariot, which flies*
et dans la nuit fuit!	*and recedes into the night!*
Autour de moi toute ma cour court,	*Around me, all my court races,*
chantant le plaisir et l'amour!	*singing of pleasure and love!*
La troupe folle des lutins	*The impish band of sprites*
suit mon char qui vole	*follows my chariot, which flies*
et dans la nuit fuit	*and recedes into the night*
au rayon de Phœbé, qui luit!	*at Phoebus' ray, which gleams!*
Parmi les fleurs	*Among the flowers*
que l'aurore fait éclore,	*which daybreak brings to bloom,*
par les bois et	*through the woods and*
par les prés diaprés,	*through the multi-colored meadows,*
sur les flots couverts d'écume,	*over the waves topped with foam,*
dans la brume, on me voit	*in the mist, one sees me*
d'un pied léger voltiger!	*light-footedly fluttering about!*
D'un pied léger,	*Light-footedly,*
par les bois, par les prés,	*through the wood and through the meadows,*
et dans la brume,	*and in the mist,*
on me voit voltiger!	*I am seen fluttering about!*
Ah! Voilà Titania!	*Ah, there's Titania!*

HAMLET

1868
music by Ambroise Thomas
libretto by Jules Barbier and Michel Carré (after the tragedy by William Shakespeare)

À vos jeux, mes amis…Partagez-vous mes fleurs!
(Ophelia's Mad Scene)

from Act IV
setting: near Elsinore in the kingdom of Denmark; amidst willows near a lake
character: Ophélie

Ophelia (Ophélie) has been driven insane by Hamlet's seeming desertion of her. She enters the stage as a strange white figure with flowing hair and a torn white dress. She addresses the peasants, telling them about a lark she heard at dawn and asking them to listen to her song.

À vos jeux, mes amis,
permettez-moi, de grâce,
de prendre part!
Nul n'a suivi ma trace!

J'ai quitté le palais
aux premiers feux du jour.
Des larmes de la nuit
la terre était mouillée;
et l'alouette, avant l'aube éveillée,
planait dans l'air!
Mais vous, pourquoi vous parlez bas?
Ne me reconnaissez-vous pas?
Hamlet est mon époux...
et je suis Ophélie!
Un doux serment nous lie,
il m'a donné son cœur
en échange du mien...
et si quelqu'un vous dit
qu'il me fuit et m'oublie,
n'en croyez rien!
N'en croyez rien; non,
Hamlet est mon époux et moi,
je suis Ophélie.
S'il trahissait sa foi,
j'en perdrais la raison!

Partagez-vous mes fleurs!
À toi cette humble branche
de romarin sauvage. Ah!
À toi cette pervenche... Ah!

Et maintenant, écoutez ma chanson!
Pâle et blonde
dort sous l'eau profonde
la Willis au regard de feu!
Que Dieu garde
celui qui s'attarde
dans la nuit, au bord du lac bleu!
Heureuse l'épouse
aux bras de l'époux!
Mon âme est jalouse
d'un bonheur si doux!
Nymphe au regard de feu,
hélas, tu dors sous
les eaux du lac bleu!
Ah! ah! ah!...La, la, la...
La sirène passe et vous entraîne
sous l'azur du lac endormi.

L'air se voile;
adieu, blanche étoile!
Adieu ciel,
adieu doux ami!
Sous les flots endormi, ah,
pour toujours, adieu, mon doux ami!
Ah! ah! ah!...La, la, la...
Ah, cher époux!
Ah, cher amant!
Ah, doux aveu!
Ah, tendre serment!
Bonheur suprême!
Ah! Cruel! Je t'aime!
Ah, cruel, tu vois mes pleurs!
Ah, pour toi je meurs!
Ah, je meurs!

In your games, my friends,
permit me, please,
to take part!
No one has followed my steps!

I left the palace
at the first light of day.
With tears from the night
the ground was damp;
and the lark, awakened before the dawn,
soared in the air!
But you, why do you whisper?
Do you not recognize me?
Hamlet is my husband...
and I am Ophelia!
A sweet oath binds us;
he has given me his heart
in exchange for mine...
and if anyone tells you
that he shuns me and forgets me,
believe nothing of it!
Believe nothing of it; no,
Hamlet is my husband and I,
I am Ophelia.
If he betrayed his faith,
I would lose my reason!

Share my flowers amongst you!
To you, this humble branch
of wild rosemary, ah!
To you this periwinkle... Ah!

And now, listen to my song!
Pale and fair-haired
sleeps, beneath the deep water,
the Willi with eyes of fire!
May God protect
the one who lingers
in the night, on the shore of the blue lake!
Happy is the wife
in the arms of her husband!
My soul is jealous
of a happiness so sweet!
Nymph with eyes of fire,
alas, you are sleeping beneath
the waters of the blue lake!
Ah, ah, ah...La, la la...
The siren passes and draws you
beneath the blue of the sleeping lake.

The sky clouds over;
farewell, white star!
Farewell, heaven;
farewell, sweet friend!
Beneath the sleeping waves, ah,
forever, farewell, my sweet friend!
Ah, ah, ah...La, la la...
Ah, dear husband!
Ah, dear lover!
Ah, sweet vow!
Ah, tender promise!
Happiness supreme!
Ah! Cruel one! I love you!
Ah, cruel one, you see my tears!
Ah, for you I die!
Ah, I am dying!

DIE FLEDERMAUS
(The Bat)
1874
music by Johann Strauss
libretto by Carl Haffner and Richard Genée (after a French vaudeville, *Le Réveillon*, by Meilhac and Halévy)

Mein Herr Marquis

from Act II
setting: Vienna, in the second half of the 19th century; a ballroom; a lavish party hosted by the Russian Prince Orlofsky
character: Adele

Gabriel von Eisenstein, a wealthy man about town, is supposed to be in jail, but he appears at Orlofsky's party disguised as the Marquis de Renard. Adele, the chambermaid in the Eisenstein household, also appears there in one of her mistress' dresses having received an invitation by her sister who is in the ballet appearing at the event. When Eisenstein suggests that she is a chambermaid everybody laughs, and Adele proceeds to make sport of her employer.

Mein Herr Marquis, ein Mann wie Sie	*My lord marquis, a man like you*
sollt' besser das versteh'n!	*should understand this better!*
Darum rate ich,	*Therefore I advise you*
ja genauer sich die Leute anzuseh'n!	*to look at people more closely!*
Die Hand ist doch wohl gar zu fein, ah,	*My hand is indeed much too delicate, ah—*
dies Füßchen so zierlich und klein, ah.	*this little foot so graceful and tiny, ah.*
Die Sprache, die ich führe,	*The language that I speak,*
die Taille, die Tournüre,	*my waistline, my shape—*
dergleichen finden Sie bei einer Zofe nie!	*the likes of which you'll never find in a chambermaid!*
Gestehen müssen Sie fürwahr:	*You must truly admit:*
sehr komisch dieser Irrtum war.	*this mistake was very funny.*
Ja, sehr komisch, ha ha ha,	*Yes, very funny, ha ha ha,*
ist die Sache, ha ha ha!	*is the thing, ha ha ha!*
Drum verzeih'n Sie, ha ha ha,	*Therefore forgive me, ha ha ha,*
wenn ich lache, ha ha ha..!	*if I laugh, ha ha ha..!*
Ach, sehr komisch, Herr Marquis, sind Sie!	*Oh my, very funny, lord marquis, you are!*
Mit dem Profil im griech'schen Stil	*With a profile in the Grecian style*
beschenkte mich Natur.	*nature has endowed me.*
Wenn nicht dies Gesicht	*If this face doesn't*
schon genügend spricht,	*already say enough,*
so seh'n Sie die Figur!	*then observe my figure!*
Schau'n durch die Lorgnette Sie dann, ah,	*Then just gaze through your lorgnette, ah,*
sich diese Toilette nur an, ah.	*at this party dress, ah.*
Mir scheinet wohl, die Liebe	*It certainly seems to me that love*
macht Ihre Augen trübe;	*is making your eyes blurry;*
Der schönen Zofe Bild	*the image of a pretty chambermaid*
hat ganz Ihr Herz erfüllt!	*has completely filled your heart!*
Nun sehen Sie sie überall;	*Now you see her everywhere;*
sehr komisch ist fürwahr der Fall.	*very funny, indeed, is the situation.*
Ja, sehr komisch...	*Yes, very funny...*

Spiel' ich die Unschuld vom Lande

from Act III
setting: Vienna, in the second half of the 19th century; a jail
character: Adele

Frank, the governor of the prison, was a guest at Orlofsky's house where he met and wooed Adele. He is feeling the effects of the night before when Adele and her sister enter. Adele, who has never performed in public but feels she is an artist by nature, comes to see if Frank will help her to get a start on her stage career, as he suggested he might, at the party. This piece is often called the "Audition Aria."

Spiel' ich die Unschuld vom Lande,	If I play the simple country girl—
natürlich im kurzen Gewande,	naturally, in a short dress—
so hüpf' ich ganz neckisch umher,	then I skip about quite roguishly,
als ob ich ein Eichkatzerl wär'!	as though I were a little squirrel!
Und kommt ein saub'rer, junger Mann,	And if a fine young man comes along,
so blinzle ich lächelnd ihn an,	then I wink, smiling, at him—
durch die Finger zwar nur,	not too seriously, to be sure—
als ein Kind der Natur,	like a child of nature,
und zupf' an meinem Schürzenband;	and tug at my apronstring;
so fängt man d'Spatzen	that's how one snares the sparrows
auf dem Land.	in the country.
Und folgt er mir, wohin ich geh',	And should he follow me wherever I go,
sag' ich naiv: Sö Schlimmer, Sö!	I say, naively, "You naughty man, you!"
Setz' mich zu ihm ins Gras sodann	I sit down by him on the grass after all
und fang' auf d'letzt zu singen an:	and begin, eventually, to sing:
la la la la..!	la la la la..!
Wenn Sie das gesehn,	Could you see this,
müssen Sie gestehn,	you'd have to admit
es wär' der Schaden nicht gering,	it would be a great misfortune
wenn mit dem Talent,	if, with my talent,
ich nicht zum Theater ging!	I didn't go on the stage!
Spiel' ich eine Königin,	If I play a queen,
schreit' ich majestätisch hin!	I stride along majestically!
Nicke hier und nicke da,	I nod from time to time,
ja ganz in meiner Gloria!	utterly in my glory!
Alles macht voll Ehrfurcht mir Spalier,	Everyone, full of awe, makes way for me
lauscht den Tönen meines Sang's.	[and] listens to the tones of my singing.
Lächelnd ich das Reich und Volk regier',	Smiling, I rule the kingdom and people:
Königin par excellence!	queen "par excellence"!
La la la la..!	La la la la..!
Wenn Sie das gesehn,	Could you see this,
werden Sie gestehn, usw.	you'd admit, etc.
Spiel' ich'ne Dame von Paris, ah,	If I play a lady from Paris, ah,
die Gattin eines Herrn Marquis, ah,	the wife of a lord marquis, ah,
da kommt ein junger Graf in's Haus, ah,	there comes a young count to the house, ah,
der geht auf meine Tugend aus, ah!	who aims at bending my virtue, ah!
Zwei Akt' hindurch geb' ich nicht nach,	Throughout two acts I don't give in,
doch ach, im dritten werd' ich schwach;	but, alas, in the third I weaken;
da öffnet plotzlich sich die Tür.	then suddenly the door flies open.
O weh, mein Mann! Was wird aus mir!	Oh woe, my husband! What will become of me!
Ah!	Ah!
Verzeihung flöt' ich;	I chirp a pardon;
er verzeiht.	he pardons.
Ah, zum Schlußtableau,	Ah, at the final tableau
da weinen d'Leut, ah, ja!	then the people are weeping—ah, yes!

THE PIRATES OF PENZANCE
or The Slave of Duty
1879
music by Arthur Sullivan
libretto by William Schwenck Gilbert

Poor wand'ring one

from Act I
setting: a rocky shore on the coast of Cornwall
character: Mabel

A group of girls, all wards of Major-General Stanley, happen on the rocky coast where only moments before a band of pirates were in conclave. Frederic, one of their number who this day ends his apprenticeship to the pirates and plans to leave them, sees the girls and is astonished by their beauty. He addresses them and hopes that one of them will look upon him with affection. The virtuous young maidens all refuse, except for Mabel.

LES CONTES D'HOFFMANN
(The Tales of Hoffmann)
1881
music by Jacques Offenbach
libretto by Jules Barbier and Michel Carré (after stories by E. T. A. Hoffmann)

The opera was unfinished at the time of Offenbach's death in 1880; completed, edited and orchestrated by Ernest Guiraud and others.

Les oiseaux dans la charmille
(Doll Song)

from Act I
setting: early 19th century; the house in Paris of the inventor Spalanzani
character: Olympia

The poet Hoffmann has come to the house of the inventor Spalanzani to become his apprentice. He falls in love with a lovely creature he meets there not realizing she is a mechanical doll and a creation of his master. Spalanzani introduces the doll at a reception and speaks of her musical accomplishments. A harp is brought on stage, and she sings to its accompaniment.

Les oiseaux dans la charmille,	*The birds in the arbor,*
dans les cieux l'astre du jour,	*in the skies, the sun—*
tout parle à la jeune fille d'amour!	*everything speaks to the young girl of love!*
Ah! tout parle d'amour!	*Ah, everything speaks of love!*
Ah!	*Ah!*
Voilà la chanson gentille,	*That's the pretty song—*
la chanson d'Olympia!	*Olympia's song!*
Ah!	*Ah!*
Tout ce qui chante et résonne	*Everything that sings and resounds*
et soupire tour à tour,	*and sighs in turn*
émeut son cœur, qui frissonne d'amour!	*arouses her heart, which quivers with love!*
Ah! tout parle d'amour!	*Ah, everything speaks of love!*
Ah!	*Ah!*
Voilà la chanson mignonne,	*That's the sweet song—*
la chanson d'Olympia!	*Olympia's song!*
Ah!	*Ah!*

LAKMÉ

1883
music by Léo Delibes
libretto by Edmond Gondinet and Philippe Gille (after Pierre Loti's *Le Mariage de Loti*)

Ah! Où va la jeune indoue
(Bell Song)

from Act II
setting: India, the 19th century; a bazaar with a temple in the background
character: Lakmé

Lakmé is the daughter of Nilakantha, a fanatical Brahmin priest. She met Gérald, a British officer, when he and his friends were sightseeing and invaded the temple compound. He confessed his love for her before being rushed away by Lakmé anticipating her father's return. Nilakantha, however, sees the figure disappearing in the forest as he arrives and cries for vengeance on the one who has defiled the temple precincts.

At the bazaar the old priest demands that his daughter, whom he introduces as a traditional Hindu singer, perform so that the unknown man will be drawn to her. She tells the story in song of an Indian maiden who one day saw a stranger lost in the forest. The maiden protects him by playing on her bells, which charm the beasts of the forest. She discovers that the stranger is Vishnu, the son of Brahma, and he transports her to the heavens.

Ah!	*Ah!*
Où va la jeune indoue,	*Where does the young Hindu girl go,*
fille des parias,	*daughter of pariahs,*
quand la lune se joue	*when the moon plays about*
dans les grands mimosas?	*in the tall mimosas?*
Elle court sur la mousse	*She runs upon the moss*
et ne se souvient pas	*and does not remember*
que partout on repousse	*that, everywhere, people spurn*
l'enfant des parias.	*the child of pariahs.*
Elle court sur la mousse,	*She runs upon the moss,*
l'enfant des parias;	*the child of pariahs;*
le long des lauriers roses,	*alongside the pink laurels,*
rêvant de douces choses,	*dreaming of sweet things,*
ah! elle passe sans bruit	*ah, she passes noiselessly,*
et riant à la nuit!	*laughing at the night!*
Là-bas dans la forêt plus sombre,	*Over there in the gloomier forest,*
quel est ce voyageur perdu?	*who is that traveller, astray?*
Autour de lui	*All around him*
des yeux brillent dans l'ombre;	*eyes sparkle in the darkness;*
il marche encore au hasard, éperdu!	*he continues walking haphazardly, bewildered!*
Les fauves rugissent de joie.	*The wild animals roar with joy.*
Ils vont se jeter sur leur proie.	*They are about to fall upon their prey.*
La jeune fille accourt	*The girl comes rushing up*
et brave leurs fureurs.	*and defies their fury.*
Elle a dans sa main la baguette	*She has in her hand the wand*
où tinte la clochette	*on which jingles the little bell*
des charmeurs.	*of magicians.*
Ah! ah! ah! ah! ah! ah! ah!	*Ah! ah! ah! ah! ah! ah! ah!*
L'étranger la regarde;	*The stranger looks at her;*
elle reste éblouie.	*she stops, dazed.*
Il est plus beau que les rajahs!	*He is more handsome than the rajahs!*
Il rougira	*He will blush with shame*
s'il sait qu'il doit la vie	*if he knows that he owes his life*
à la fille des parias.	*to the daughter of pariahs.*
Mais lui, l'endormant dans un rêve,	*But he, lulling her to sleep in a dream,*
jusque dans le ciel il l'enlève,	*raises her up into heaven,*
en lui disant: ta place est là!	*telling her: your place is there!*
C'était Vichnou, fils de Brahma!	*It was Vishnu, son of Brahma!*

24

Depuis ce jour, au fond des bois,	Since that day, in the depths of the woods,
le voyageur entend parfois	the traveller sometimes hears
le bruit léger de la baguette	the faint sound of the wand
où tinte la clochette	on which jingles the little bell
des charmeurs.	of magicians.
Ah!	Ah!

ZOLOTOJ PETUSHOK
(Le Coq d'Or)
The Golden Cockerel
1909
music by Nikolai Rimsky-Korsakov
libretto by Vladimir Bel'skii (after a fairy tale by Pushkin)

Otvet' mne, zorkoe svetilo (Hymn to the Sun)

from Act II
setting: a narrow and desolate mountain pass in the kingdom of King Dodon
character: Shemakhanskaja tsaritsa (the Queen of Shemakha)

Dodon's kingdom is constantly besieged, and at last an astrologer offers the king a magic golden cockerel that will crow in warning of an attack. It's not long before the cry of the cockerel is heard, and Dodon prepares for a war that goes badly. His sons are slain and as he concludes his lament over their bodies the mists rise and reveal an elaborate tent. Dodon's men fire upon it but the only effect is that a ravishingly beautiful young woman emerges from the tent resplendently gowned and wearing a white turban with a long feather. Followed by four slaves with musical instruments she raises her arms in invocation and intones the "Hymn to the Sun."

Otvet' mne, zorkoe svetilo,	Answer me, vigilant dawn.
S vostoka k nam prikhodish' ty:	You come to us from the East.
Moj kraj rodnoj ty posetilo,	Have you visited my native land,
Otchiznu skazochnoj mechty?	the motherland of a fairytale dream?
Vsë tak zhe l' tam sijajut rozy	Are there still roses beaming there
I lilij ognennykh kusty?	and bushes of fiery lilies?
I birjuzovye strekozy	And turquoise dragonflies
Lobzajut pyshnye listy?	kissing the luxurious leaves?
I v vecheru u vodoëma	And in the evening by the pond
V nesmelykh pesnjakh dev i zhën,	in timid songs of maidens and women,
Vsë ta zhe l' divnaja istoma,	is there still the same divine languor,
Ljubvi zapretnoj strastnyj son?	a passionate dream of forbidden love?
Vsë tak zhe l' dorog gost' sluchajnyj	Is the unexpected guest still dear?
Emu gotovy i dary	Are the gifts prepared for him,
I skromnyj pir, i vzgljad potajnyj,	and a modest feast, and a secret glance
Skvoz' tkan' revnivuju chadry?	through the fabric of a jealous chadra?
A noch' sgustitsja golubaja,	While the blue night deepens,
K nemu, zabyv i styd, i strakh,	to him, having forgotten the shame and fear,
Speshit khozjajka molodaja	is a young mistress hurrying
S priznan'em sladostnym v ustakh?	with a sweet confession on her lips?

Russian translation and transliteration by Carol Reynolds

ARIADNE AUF NAXOS
1912, revised 1916
music by Richard Strauss
libretto by Hugo von Hofmannsthal (after Hofmannsthal's German translation of Molière's play, *Le Bourgeois Gentilhomme*)

Großmächtige Prinzessin…Noch glaub' ich dem einen ganz mich gehörend

in one act
setting: Vienna, the 18th century; a stage setting representing the isle of Naxos in ancient Greece
character: Zerbinetta

At the great house of a wealthy patron of the arts, an opera company and a comedia dell'arte troupe are preparing separate works for an evening's entertainment. To the horror of the opera composer, whose new work is based on the Greek legend of Ariadne abandoned on the island of Naxos, all the artists are informed that they must perform both stageworks simultaneously in order to finish on time for the royal fireworks. The composer is persuaded to fuse his work with that of the comedians. The opera within an opera begins.

At a cave in Naxos Ariadne, now deserted by her lover Theseus, calls upon death to ease her suffering. Zerbinetta and the other commedia dell'arte characters enter and try to cheer Ariadne with song and dance. When that fails, Zerbinetta lingers at the cave to persuade Ariadne more candidly. She expounds on her philosophy that love may come and love may go, but a girl must be prepared to move on.

Großmächtige Prinzessin,	High and mighty princess,
wer verstünde nicht,	who wouldn't understand
daß so erlauchter und erhabener Personen	that for such noble and lofty persons
Traurigkeit mit einem anderen Maas gemessen	sadness must be measured with another
werden muß,	standard
als der gemeinen Sterblichen.	than for ordinary mortals.
Jedoch, sind wir nicht Frauen unter uns,	And yet, are we not both women,
und schlägt denn nicht in jeder Brust	and does there not beat in each breast
ein unbegreiflich Herz?	an inexplicable heart?
Von unsrer Schwachheit sprechen,	To speak of our weakness,
sie uns selber eingestehn,	to admit it to ourselves—
ist es nicht schmerzlich süß?	is it not painfully sweet?
Und zuckt uns nicht der Sinn danach?	And do our senses not thrill from it?
Sie wollen mich nicht hören...	You do not wish to hear me...
schön und stolz und regungslos,	Beautiful and proud and motionless,
als wären Sie die Statue	as though you were the statue
auf Ihrer eignen Gruft.	on your own tomb.
Sie wollen keine andere Vertraute	Do you want to have no other confidante
als diesen Fels und diese Wellen haben?	than this rock and these waves?
Prinzessin, hören Sie mich an—	Princess, listen to me:
nicht Sie allein, wir alle ach,	not for you alone—all of us, ah,
wir alle was ihr Herz erstarrt…	for all of us that which numbs the heart...
wer ist die Frau,	who is the woman
die es nicht durchgelitten hätte?	who has not suffered through it?
Verlassen! in Verzweiflung! ausgesetzt!	Forsaken! In despair! Rejected!
Ach, solcher wüsten Inseln	Ah, such desolate islands
sind unzählige auch mitten unter Menschen,	are countless even among men.
ich, ich selber habe ihrer mehrere bewohnt	I myself have inhabited many of them,
und habe nicht gelernt, die Männer zu verfluchen.	and have not learned to curse men.
Treulos sie sinds!	Faithless—they are that!
Ungeheuer, ohne Grenzen!	Monstrous, without limits!
Eine kurze Nacht, ein hastiger Tag,	A brief night, a passionate day,
ein Wehen der Luft,	a flutter of the breeze,
ein fließender Blick verwandelt ihr Herz!	a fleeting glance transforms their hearts!
Aber sind wir denn gefeit gegen die grausamen,	But are we protected against the cruel,
entzückenden, die unbegreiflichen Verwandlungen?	delightful, incredible transformations?
Noch glaub' ich dem einen ganz	Yet when I believe myself belonging
mich gehörend,	to one man,
noch mein' ich mir selber so sicher zu sein,	and think myself to be so trustworthy,
da mischt sich im Herzen	there mingle in my heart,
leise betörend	gently infatuating,
schon einer nie gekosteten Freiheit,	feelings of a never-tasted freedom,

26

schon einer neuen verstohlenen Liebe
schweifendes, freches Gefühle sich ein.
Noch bin ich wahr und doch ist es gelogen,
ich halte mich treu und bin schon schlecht,
mit falschen Gewichten wird alles gewogen
und halb mich wissend
und halb im Taumel
betrüg ich ihn endlich
und lieb ihn nocht recht.

So war es mit Pagliazzo und Mezzetin!
Dann war es Cavicchio, dann Burattin,
dann Pasquariello!
Ach und zuweilen will es mir scheinen,
waren es zwei!
Doch niemals Launen, immer ein Müssen,
immer ein neues beklommenes Staunen:
daß ein Herz sogar sich selber nicht versteht.

Als ein Gott kam Jeder gegangen
und sein Schritt schon machte mich stumm,
küßte er mir Stirn und Wangen,
war ich von dem Gott gefangen
und gewandelt um und um.
Als ein Gott kam Jeder gegangen,
Jeder wandelte mich um,
küßte er mir Mund und Wangen,
hingegeben war ich stumm.
Kam der neue Gott gegangen, hingegeben
war ich stumm…

of a furtive love
wandering and shameless.
So am I sincere and yet deceptive;
I consider myself true but am quite bad.
With false importance everything is weighed
and half knowing what I'm doing
and half in ecstasy
I betray him in the end
and yet really love him.

So it was with Pagliazzo and Mezzetin!
Then it was Cavicchio, then Burattin,
then Pasquariello!
Once in a while it seemed to me that
there were two!
But never whims...always a necessity,
always a new, anxious amazement:
that a heart cannot even understand itself.

Like a god each one came,
and his step made me speechless.
As he kissed my brow and cheeks
I was captivated by the god
and completely changed.
Like a god each one came,
each one transformed me.
He kissed my mouth and cheeks;
yielding, I was silent.
The new god came; yielding,
I was silent…

THE TELEPHONE
1947
music by Gian Carlo Menotti
libretto by the composer

Hello! Oh, Margaret, it's you

in one act
setting: United States, mid-20th century; Lucy's apartment
character: Lucy

Lucy's boyfriend Ben is about to go away, but he stops at her apartment to bring a gift and probably propose marriage. He seems on the point of popping the question when the telephone rings. It's a call from Lucy's friend, Margaret, and they have a lot to say.

THE TEMPEST
1986
music by Lee Hoiby
libretto by Mark Shulgasser (after the play by William Shakespeare)

Vocalise

from Act II, scene 2
setting: legendary; a remote island
character: Ariel, an airy spirit

Some years before, Prospero, Duke of Milan, and his daughter Miranda were shipwrecked on a strange island. When they arrived the island was uninhabited save for spirits and the creature Caliban, half fish and half man, who is the son of the witch Sycorax. Prospero released the spirits imprisoned by Sycorax from bondage, but retained the service of one, Ariel. After another shipwreck and the clamor of a silent world suddenly occupied by many, Ariel begins the second scene of Act II alone, suspended from a cloud and giving voice to the night air and the moonlight.

Tornami a vagheggiar
from
ALCINA

George Frideric Handel

MORGANA:

Tor - na-mi a va-gheg -

giar, _____ te so - lo vuol a - mar _____ quest' a - ni - ma fe -

del, _____ ca - ro _____ mio be -

ne, ca - ro,

tor - na - mi a va - gheg - giar.

Tor - na - mi a va - gheg - giar,

te so - lo vuol a -

mar, te so - lo vuol a - mar

quest' a - ni - ma fe - del, ca - ro mi - o be - ne,

te so - lo vuol a - mar

quest' a - ni - ma fe - del, ca - ro mi-o be - ne, ca - - - ro,____ ca - ro___ mio be - ne.

[VI-]*

* Suggested cut for auditions.

Già ti do - nai il mio cor, già ti do - nai il mio

Durch Zärtlichkeit und Schmeicheln
from
DIE ENTFÜHRUNG AUS DEM SERAIL

Wolfgang Amadeus Mozart

BLONDE:

Durch Zärt-lich-keit _ und _ Schmei-cheln, Ge-fäl-lig-keit _ und _ Scher-zen er-o-bert man _ die _ Her-zen der gu-ten _ Mäd-chen leicht, _ der

gu - ten Mäd - chen leicht. Doch

mür - ri - sches Be - feh - len, und

Pol - tern, Zan - ken, Pla - gen, und

Pol - tern, Zan - ken, Pla - gen macht,

daß in we - nig Ta - gen so __ Lieb' als Treu' ent -

weicht, __ macht, __ daß in we - nig Ta - gen so __

Lieb' __ als __ Treu' ent - weicht, _____

fp

so

Lieb' als Treu' entweicht. Durch Zärtlichkeit und

Schmeicheln, Gefälligkeit und Scherzen er-

obert man die Herzen der guten Mädchen

leicht, der guten Mädchen leicht. Doch mürrisches Be-

Da schlägt die Abschiedsstunde

from
DER SCHAUSPIELDIREKTOR

Wolfgang Amadeus Mozart

MADAME HERZ:

Da schlägt die Ab-schieds-stun - de, um grau - sam uns zu tren-nen, um grau - sam, um grau - sam uns zu tren-nen. Wie werd' ich le - ben kön - nen, o

*Appoggiatura recommended

Da - mon, oh - ne dich, oh - ne dich?

sf *p*

cresc. *f* *p*

Ich will _ dich be - glei - ten,

im Geist _ dir zur Sei - ten   schwe - ben   um ___

dich, ___   schwe - ben   um   dich.   Und

sf   *sf*   *p*

Allegro moderato

sein.
Ein Herz, das so __ der Ab - schied

krän-ket, dem ist kein Wan - kel -mut _ be-kannt, kein Wan - kel -mut be-

kannt!
Wo-hin es auch _ das Schick - sal len - ket,

nichts trennt das fest - ge - knüpf - te Band, nichts trennt ____

44

nichts trennt _ das fest -

- ge-knüpf - te Band, ___ das fest - ge - knüpf - te _ Band. Wo -

hin es auch das Schick-sal len - ket, nichts trennt das fest - ge - knüpf-te

Band, das _ fest - ge - knüpf - te Band.

pp

O zittre nicht, mein lieber Sohn

from
DIE ZAUBERFLÖTE

Wolfgang Amadeus Mozart

Allegro maestoso

KÖNIGIN DER NACHT:

O zit-tre nicht, mein lie-ber Sohn;

du bist un-schul-dig,

Larghetto

wei - se, fromm. Ein Jüng - ling, so wie du, ver - mag am

bes - ten das tief - be - trüb - te Mut - ter - herz zu trö - sten.

Zum Lei - den bin ich aus - er - ko - ren; denn mei - ne

Toch - ter feh - let mir. Durch sie ging all mein Glück ver - lo - ren, durch

sie ging all mein Glück ver - lo - ren; ein Bö - se-wicht, ein

Bö - se-wicht ent-floh mit ihr. Noch seh'__ ich ihr

Zit - tern mit ban - gem Er - schüt - tern, ihr

ängst - li - ches Be - ben, ihr schüch - ter - nes

50

52

e - - - - wig
auf

dein,   auf   e - wig   dein,   auf

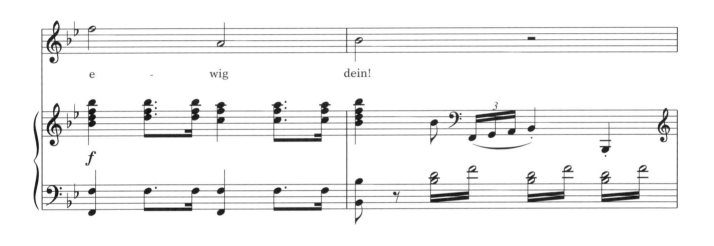

e - wig   dein!

Der Hölle Rache
from
DIE ZAUBERFLÖTE

Wolfgang Amadeus Mozart

so bist du mei - ne Toch - ter

fp *fp* *fp* *cresc.*

nim - mer - mehr!

f

p

f *p*

Ver - stoß - en sei auf

Hört,   hört,   hört,

Ra - che -

göt - ter!   Hört   der Mut - ter Schwur!

Plus de dépit, plus de tristesse

from
LES DEUX AVARES

André Grétry

chan - - - - - - -

te quand je ___ te ___ vois. Plus de dé - pit,

p

plus de ___ tris - tes - se, dès ___ que ___ je ___ puis vo -

Una voce poco fa
from
IL BARBIERE DI SIVIGLIA

Gioachino Rossini

The original key is E major. The transposition up to F is traditional for coloratura sopranos.

68

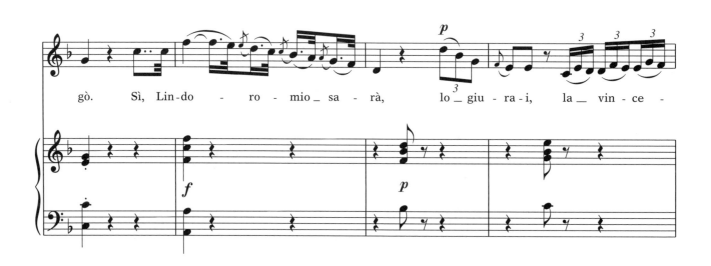

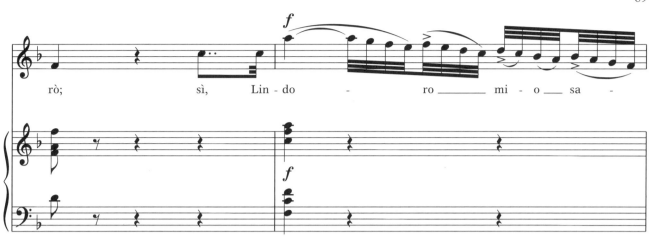

rò; sì, Lin - do - ro _____ mi - o - sa -

rà, lo giu - ra - i, ah _____ la vin - ce -

rà, lo giu - ra - i, la _ vin - ce - rò.

Il tu-tor ri -cu-se - rà, io l'in-ge - gno a-guz-ze -

70

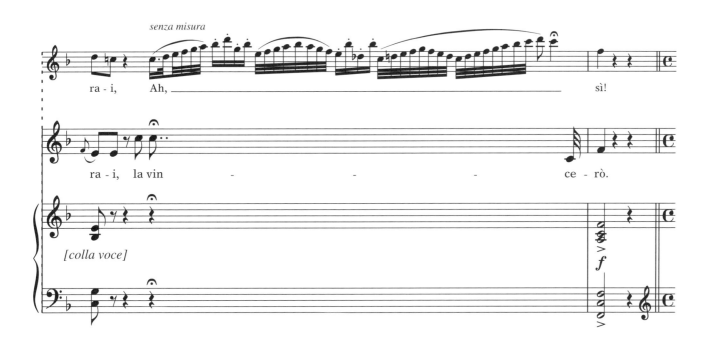

Allegro moderato

72

Io so - no do - ci - le,

son __ ri - spet - to - sa, so - no ub - bi -

dien - te, dol - ce, a - mo - ro - sa; mi la-scio

reg - ge-re, mi la-scio reg - ge-re, mi fò gui-dar, mi ___ fò ___ gui-

dar. ___ Ma, ma se mi

dar. ___ Ma se mi toc - ca-no dov'-è il mio de - bo-le, sa-rò u-na

74

rò _____ gio -

trap - po _____ le fa - rò, fa - rò gio -

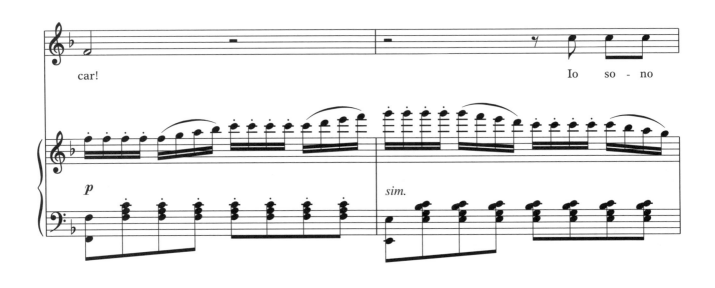

car!   Io so - no

do - ci - le,   so - no ub - bi -

dien - te, mi la - scio reg - ge-re, mi fò gui -

dar. Ma, ma se mi

dar. Ma se mi

toc - ca - no, ah, dov' - è il mio de - bo - le, ah, sa - rò u - na

toc - ca - no dov' - è il mio de - bo - le, sa - rò u - na

78

vi - pe - ra, _____ sa - rò; _____ e cen - to

vi - pe - ra, _____ sa - rò; e cen - to

trap - po - le, ah, ah, pri - ma di ce - de - re, ah, ah, fa - rò gio -

trap - po - le, pri - ma di ce - de - re, fa - rò gio -

a piacere

car, _____ e cen - to

a piacere

car, _____ fa - rò _____ gio - car; e cen - to

col canto

80

car, fa - rò gio - car;

car, fa - rò gio - car, fa - rò gio -

f

rall. *senza misura*

Ah, _____ sì!

a tempo

car, _ fa - rò

gio - car.

f

a tempo

ff

Ah! non credea... Ah! non giunge

from

LA SONNAMBULA

Vincenzo Bellini

AMINA:

Ah! non cre-dea mi - rar - ti sì pre - sto e-stin-to, o

fio - re; pas-sa - sti al par_ d'a-mo - re, che un gior - no

so - lo, che un gior - no sol_ du - rò,_____ che un gior - no

so - lo, ah! _ sol du - rò.

Pas - sa - sti al par d'a-mo - re,

che un gior - no, che un gior - no sol du -

rò. Po - tria no-vel _ vi -

ten - to _____ on - d'i - o son _ pie - na: a' miei sen - si _____ io cre - do ap -

pe - na; _____ tu m'af - fi - da, _____ o _ mi - o te - sor! Ah! mi ab -

brac - cia, e sem - pre in - sie - me, sem - pre u - ni - ti _____ in u - na

spe - me, del - la ter - ra _____ in cui vi - via - mo _____ ci for -

88

Allegro moderato

Ah! non giun - ge _____ u-man pen-sie - ro _____ al con -

pp *leggierissimo*

ossia

pie - na, a' miei

ten - to _____ on - d'i-o son _ pie - na, a' miei sen - si _____ io cre - do ap -

mor, ah

via - mo ci for - mia - mo un ciel d'a - mor, d'a -

d'a -

mor, d'a - mor, d'a -

col canto

Più vivo

mor!

f   ff

* Optional cadenza:

(mor,) _____ Ah _____ d'a-mor!

Care compagne... Come per me sereno

from
LA SONNAMBULA

Vincenzo Bellini

Recitativo

AMINA:

Ca - re com - pa - gne, e vo - i, te - ne - ri a - mi - ci che al - la gio - ia mi - a tan - ta par - te pren - de - te, oh co - me dol - ci scen - don d'A - mi - na al co - re i can - ti che v'in - spi - ra il _____ vo - stro a - mo - re!

[p]

pp

pp

A te, di - let - ta, te - ne - ra ma - dre, che a sì lie - to

gior - no me or - fa - nel - la ser - ba - sti, a te fa - vel - li que - sto, dal

cor ___ più che dal ci - glio e - spres - so, dol - ce pian - to di gio - ia, dol - ce

Andante con anima

pian - to di gio - ia, e que - st'am - ples - so.

94

Moderato

So - vra il sen la ___ man mi

po - sa; pal - pi - tar, bal - zar, ___ bal - zar lo ___ sen - ti: e - gli è il

di forza

cor che_ i_ suoi con - ten - ti non ha for - za a so - ste - ner,

98

Ca - ri a - mi - ci,

a - ma - ta ma-dre!

[senza misura]

Ah!

99

102

* optional tacet until page 105, 2nd system

zar, bal - zar, bal -

Ah

zar, bal - zar, bal -

zar!

105

Regnava nel silenzio
from
LUCIA DI LAMMERMOOR

Gaetano Donizetti

Larghetto

LUCIA:

Re - gna - va nel __ si - len - zio al - ta la not - te e

bru - na... col pia la fon - te un pal - li - do

rag - gio _ di _ te - tra lu - na... quan-do un som - mes - so

senza misura

for - to, ah, ___ è con-for - to al ___

rall.

for - to, è con-for - to al ___ mi - o, al mi - o pe -

col canto   colla voce

Moderato

nar.

112

col fa - vel-lar del co - re _____ mi giu - ra e-ter - na

fè, gli af - fan - ni mie - i di - men - ti-co;

gio - ia di - vie - ne ___ il pian - to.

[rall.]   col canto

a tempo

Par - mi _____ che a lu - i d'ac-can - to si

114

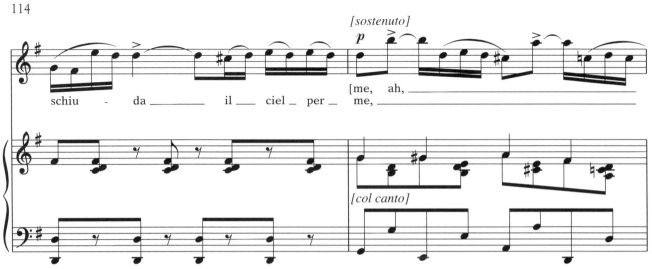

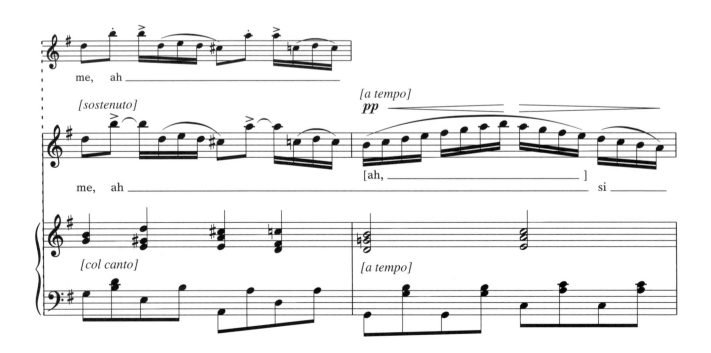

ciel _____ per _____

schiu - da _ il _ ciel _____ per _____ me.

Poco più mosso

f

[*tr* ~~~~~~]

rall. e cresc.

Ah! _____

rall.   *p*

118

si schiu - da il ciel per

me, ah, ah,

me, si

per me.

schiu - da il ciel per me. A

*Traditional cut

lui d'ac - can - to si schiu-da _____ il ciel _____ per _____ me, ah! _____ si _____ schiu - da il ciel, il ciel per me. A

Il dolce suono... Spargi d'amaro pianto

(Mad Scene)

from

LUCIA DI LAMMERMOOR

Gaetano Donizetti

Il dol - ce suo - no mi col-pì di sua vo - ce. Ah, quel-la

vo - ce m'è qui nel cor di - sce - sa. Ed - gar - do, io ti son

Ed - gar - do! Ed - gar - do!

ah!

f spaventata

Il _____ fan - ta-sma, il _____ fan -

p

Recit.

ta-sma ne se - pa - - ra! Qui ri - co-vria-mo, Ed -

col canto

piè _____ del - l'a - - ra.

gar - do, a piè _____ del - l'a - - ra.

* Appoggiatura possible

* Appoggiatura possible

130

132

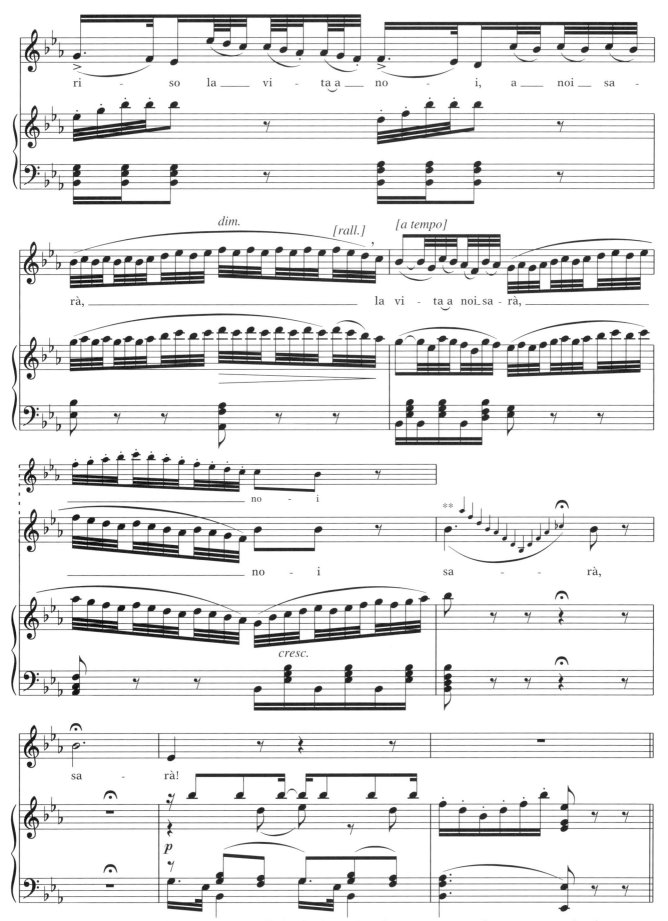

** A cadenza accompanied by flute traditionally begins here. See the next two pages for two suggested cadenzas which replace these four bars.

134

Cadenza I *
senza misura

* a cadenza used by Lily Pons and others

136

Moderato

p

sim.

a tempo

p *a tempo* *sim.*

Spar - gi d'a - ma - ro pian - to il mio ter - re - stre

ve - lo, men - tre las - sù nel cie -

138

142

Ah!

[Ah!
Ah!

O rendetemi la speme... Qui la voce

from
I PURITANI

Vincenzo Bellini

146

scia - te, la-scia - te-mi mo _ rir, _ o ren-de - te-mi _ la _ spe - me, _____ o la-scia - te, la-scia - te-mi mo - rir. _

Allegro

148

149

po - sa vien, ti po - sa sul mio cor! Deh! t'af-fret - ta, _____ o Ar-tu - ro

mi - o, rie - di, o ca - ro, _____ al - la tua El - vi - ra: es - sa

pian - ge e _____ ti so - spi - ra. Vien, _____ o ca - ro, al - l'a -

mo - re, vien _____ al - l'a -

152

Ah, tardai troppo...
O luce di quest'anima

from
LINDA DI CHAMOUNIX

Gaetano Donizetti

LINDA: Recitative

Ah, tar-dai trop-po, e al no-stro fa-vo-ri-to con-ve-gno io non tro-va-i il mio di-let-to Car-lo. E chi sa ma-i quant' e-gli a-vrà sof-

*Apoggiatura recommended

co - ra, e - gli s'in-nal -ze - rà   co' suoi ta - len -ti!   Sa - rò sua spo-sa al -

col canto

ossia

con - ten - - - ti!

lo - ra... Oh no i con -ten - - ti!

Allegretto

che te so-spi-ra e bra - ma, che per te sol vi - vrà!

O lu - ce di quest' a - ni - ma, a - mor, de - li - zia e

vi - ta, u - ni - ta no-stra sor -

- te in ter-ra in ciel sa - rà, u - ni - ta no-stra sor - te

O — lu – ce — di quest' a – ni – ma,

a tempo

O lu – ce di quest' a – ni – ma,

a tempo

pp

de – li – zia, a – mo – re e vi – ta,

de – li – zia, a – mo – re e vi – ta,

calando

la no-stra sor-te u – ni – ta in ter-ra, in ciel sa – rà.

p

calando

p

Deh vie-ni a me, ri - po-sa - ti su que-sto cor che t'a - ma,

che te so - spi - ra e bra - ma, che per te sol vi -

vra. Ah _____ O __ lu - ce __ di __ quest' __

vra _____ O lu - ce di quest'

164

Ah!

vie

ni.

Chacun le sait

from

LA FILLE DU RÉGIMENT

Gaetano Donizetti

La la la la la la la la la la la la. La la la la la la la la la la la la. Ah

Ah!

Cha - cun le sait, cha - cun le dit: le ré - gi - ment __ par ex - cel -

len - ce, le seul à qui l'on fass' cré - dit dans tous __ les ca - ba - rets __ de __

166

168

reur, ___ on ___ le ___ pen - se, fe - ra cha - cun de ses sol-

dats, à la ___ paix, ma - ré -chal ___ de ___ Fran - ce! Car c'est con-

nu le ___ ré - gi -ment le plus vain -queur, le ___ plus char-

mant, ___ et ___ que l'autre

mant, qu'un_ se -xe craint, et ___ que l'autre ai - me. Il est

rall.

[suivez]

170

possible cadenza, piano tacet

Quel guardo il cavaliere...
So anch'io la virtù magica
from
DON PASQUALE

Gaetano Donizetti

172

lie - re _____ in mez-zo al cor tra - fis - se;

pie - gò il gi - noc - chio e dis - se: Son vo-stro ca - va -

lier. E tan - to e - ra in quel guar - do

sa - por di pa - ra - di - so _____

176

* This cut is traditional

guor. So an-ch'io la vir - tù ma - gi-ca per in - spi-ra - re a - mor; ___ co-

no - sco l'ef - fet - to, ah _____ sì, ah _____

Ricci's optional ending:

sì! Ah! _____

(Ah!) _____

* Optional ending for the aria as advised by Ricci.

sì, per in-spi-ra - re — a - mor.

Ho te - sta biz - zar - ra, son pron-ta e vi - va - ce,

bril - la - re mi pia-ce, mi pia-ce scher - zar.   Ah, _____

mi

pia - ce, mi pia - ce scher-

zar. Ho te - sta vi - va - ce, mi pia - ce scher-

[pp]

zar. Ho te - sta vi - va - ce, mi pia - ce scher-

[f]

zar, mi pia - ce scher - zar, mi pia - ce scher-

zar. Ah, _____ mi pia - ce, mi

ossia

scher - zar! _____

pia - ce scher - zar!

Ombre légère
(Shadow Song)
from
DINORAH

Giacomo Meyerbeer

186

Allegretto ben moderato (♩. = 52)

son!

légèrement

Om-bre lé - gè - re, qui suis mes pas, ____ ne t'en va pas, _ non, non,

non! Fée ou chi - mè - re, qui m'est si chè - re, ne t'en va pas! _ Non, non,

non! Cou - rons en - sem - ble, j'ai peur, je trem - ble quand tu t'en

vas _ loin de moi! _____ Ah! _____ Ne t'en _____ va

188

ter! _____ Ap - pro - che - toi! Viens, ré - ponds -

ossia

moi! Chan - te a - vec moi! _____

Allegro animato (♩. = 92)

Ah! _____

ré-ponds! Ah! _____

190

192

194

197

Ah! _____

199

200

C'est l'histoire amoureuse
(Laughing Song)
from
MANON LESCAUT

Daniel François Esprit Auber

ris! Ah! _____

BOURBONNAISE
Allegro ♩ = 138

f

C'est l'his - toire a - mou -

p

205

reu-se, au-tant que fa-bu-leu-se, d'un ga-lant fier à bras, ah ah ah ah ah ah ah
bi-le, car dans la gran-de vil-le il est des ma-gis-trats! Ah ah ah ah ah ah ah
sai-re, a-lors que vers Cy-thè-re vous por-te-rez vos pas, ah ah ah ah ah ah ah

ah... d'un ten-dre com-mis-sai-re que l'on croy-ait sé-vè-re et qui ne l'é-tait
ah. Il est des ré-ver-bè-res van-tés pour leurs lu-miè-res et qui n'é-clai-rent
ah, Di-o-gè-ne mo-der-ne, pre-nez vo-tre lan-ter-ne, de crain-te de faux

pas! Ah ah ah ah ah ah ah ah. Il ai-mait u-ne belle, ah ah! Il en vou-lait, mais
pas! Ah ah ah ah ah ah ah ah. Au lo-gis de la belle, ah ah, un soir que sans chan-
pas! Ah ah ah ah ah ah ah ah. Mais c'est qu'à la lu-mière, ah ah, vous au-rez peine à

206

poco rit.

elle, ah ah, de lui ne vou-lait pas! Ah ah ah ah ah ah ah ah. Or, vou-lez-vous ap -
delle, ah ah, il veut por - ter ses pas, ah ah ah ah ah ah ah ah, l'es - ca - lier é - tait
plaire, ah ah! Et dès qu'on vous ver - ra, ah ah ah ah ah ah ah ah, oui, rien qu'à vo - tre

suivez

pren - dre le nom de ce Lé - an - dre, traî - tre com - me Ju -
som - bre, et sur son nez, dans l'om - bre, il tom - be! Pa - ta -
fa - ce, en fai - sant la gri - ma - ce, l'a - mour s'en - vo - le -

a tempo

das! Son nom? Vous al - lez ri - re. Je m'en vais vous le di - re bien
tras! Son nom? Vous al - lez ri - re. Je m'en vais vous le di - re bien
ra. Pour cal - mer son dé - li - re, son nom je vais le di - re bien

a tempo

la la la la la la la la la la la la la la la la. [la la la la

la.]

1,2

3

2. On le di - sait ha - la.
3. Ô ga - lant com - mis -

Den Teuren zu versöhnen

from
MARTHA

Friedrich von Flotow

LADY HARRIET: Recitative

Zum treu-en Freun-de geh', den Plan ihm zu ent-

de-cken, den mein be-reu-end Herz voll Zu-ver-sicht er-dacht, aus dump-fer Schwer-mut

Traum den Teu-ren zu er-we-cken mit neu-em Hoff-nungs-strahl, nach trü-ber Ker-ker-

210

welch Glück!

Ach! _____ den _

Teu - ren zu ver - söh - nen durch wah - re Reu', durch wah - re Reu', sein _

Da - sein zu ver - schö - nen mit Lieb' und Treu', mit Lieb' und Treu'. _

215

mein,   mein   wird   er,

p

mein,   ja   mein!

opt.

f

ff

Je suis Titania

from

MIGNON

Ambroise Thomas

218

Ah! _____ Je par-cours le mon - de,

Ah! _____ Ah! _____

Ah! _____ Ah! _____

Ah! Plus vi - ve que l'oi-

seau,   plus   prom-pte que l'é - clair!   Ah! _____

Je ____ suis Ti -ta - ni - a la

blon - de. Je ___ suis Ti -ta -ni -a, fil - le ____ de l'air! En ri-

222

ant, _____ je par - cours le mon - de plus vi - ve

que _ l'oi - seau, _ plus _ prom - pte _ que _____ l'é - clair!

Je _ suis Ti - ta - ni - a la

blon - de! Ah! _____

La trou-pe fol - le des lu - tins suit mon char qui vole et dans la nuit fuit ___

senza rigore

___ au ra - yon de Phœ -bé, qui luit! Par -

_pp_

mi ___ les fleurs que l'au - ro - re fait _ é -

_pp_

clo - re, par les bois _ et par _ les prés di - a - prés, ___

dolce

sur _____ les flots cou - verts _ d'é - cu - me, _ dans _ la _

très doux

bru - me, on me voit _ d'un pied _ lé - ger vol - ti - ger! _____

D'un pied _ lé - ger, par les bois, par les prés, et dans _ la

brume, on me voit vol-ti-ger, on me voit vol-ti-ger! Ah! _____

mf

Volta la terrea
from
UN BALLO IN MASCHERA

Giuseppe Verdi

232

Chi _____ la pro-fe-ti-ca _____ su-a gon-na af-fer - ra,

o _____ pas-si'l ma - re, _____ vo-li al-la guer - ra,

le sue vi-cen - de _____ so-a-vi,a - ma - re

À vos jeux, mes amis...
Partagez-vous mes fleurs!

(Ophelia's Mad Scene)
from
HAMLET

Ambroise Thomas

jeux, mes a - mis, per - met - tez - moi, de grâ - ce de pren-dre part!

p

3

f

Nul n'a sui-vi ma tra - ce! J'ai quit-té le pa - lais aux pre-miers feux _____ du

[Più mosso]

jour.

pp

rit.

Andantino

Des lar - mes de __ la nuit __ la terre é-tait mouil-lé - e; Et l'a-lou -

et - te, a - vant l'aube é - veil - lé - e, pla - nait dans

l'air,

suivez

poux... et je suis O-phé - li - e!

trés soutenu, à demi voix

Un doux ser-ment nous li - e, il m'a don-né son cœur en é-

pp expressif

chan - ge du mien... et si quel-qu'un vous dit

qu'il me fuit et m'ou-bli - e, qu'il me fuit et ___ m'ou - bli - e,

n'en croy-ez rien!   Si l'on vous dit _____ qu'il m'ou-bli - e,   n'en cro-yez

rien;   non, _____ Ham - let   est mon _____ é - poux et moi, _____ et   moi je suis O-phé-li -

e

S'il tra-his-sait sa foi,   j'en per-drais la rai - son!

Allegretto mouvement de valse ♩. = 58

242

gaiment

Par - ta - gez - vous mes

(à une jeune fille)

fleurs! _____

À

toi _____ cette hum - ble bran -

che de ro - ma - rin sau -

va - ge.

246

BALLADE
Andantino con moto

Et main - te - nant é - cou-tez ma chan-son!

248

feu, hé - las! tu dors sous les eaux du lac bleu!

Ah! _____ Ah! _____

Allegretto

à volonté

éclatant de rire

Ah! Ah! Ah! Ah! Ah! Ah!

Ah! _____

250

254

Ah!

Ah! ____ Ah! ____ je meurs!

*Optional cadenza

Ah! ____

____ je meurs!

Mein Herr Marquis
from
DIE FLEDERMAUS

Johann Strauss

seh'n!

gur!

Die Hand ist doch wohl gar zu fein, ah, ____

Schau'n durch die Lorg - net - te Sie dann, ah, ____

____ dies Füß - chen so zier - lich und klein, ah. ____ Die

____ sich die - se Toi - let - te nur an, ah. ____ Mir

rit.   *a tempo*

Spra - che, die ich füh - re, die Tail - le, die Tour - nü - re, der -

schei - net wohl, die Lie - be macht Ih - re Au - gen trü - be; der

cresc.   *rit.*   *p*   *a tempo*

glei - chen fin - den Sie bei ei - ner Zo - fe nie, der -

schö - nen Zo - fe Bild hat ganz Ihr Herz er - füllt, der

fz

glei - chen fin-den Sie bei ei - ner Zo - fe nie! Ge - ste - hen
schö - nen Zo - fe Bild hat ganz Ihr Herz er - füllt! Nun se - hen

müs - sen Sie für - wahr: sehr ko - misch die - ser
Sie sie ü - ber - all; sehr ko - misch ist für -

Irr - tum war. 1., 2. Ja, sehr ko - misch, ha ha ha, ist die Sa - che,

ha ha ha! Drum ver-zeih'n Sie, ha ha ha, wenn ich la - che,

Spiel' ich die Unschuld vom Lande
from
DIE FLEDERMAUS

Johann Strauss

ADELE:

Spiel' ich die Un-schuld vom Lan - de, na - tür-lich im kur-zen Ge - wan - de, so

hüpf' ich ganz neck-ish um - her, _____ als ob ich ein Eich-kat-zerl wär'! _____

Und kommt ein saub'-rer, jun - ger Mann, so blinz-le ich lä-chelnd ihn an, _____

durch die Fin-ger zwar nur, _____ als ein Kind der Na - tur, und zupf' an

mei - nem Schür - zen - band; so fängt man d'Spat - zen auf dem Land. Und

folgt er mir, wo - hin ich geh', sag' ich na - iv: Sö Schlim - mer, Sö! Setz'

mich zu ihm ins Gras so-dann und fang' auf d'letzt zu sin - gen an:

264

266

Ehr-furcht mir Spa-lier, lauscht den Tö - nen ___ mei - nes Sang's. Lä - chelnd _ ich das _

Reich und Volk re-gier', Kö - ni - gin par ex-cel-lence! La _____ la ___

la la la la la la _ la _ la la ____ la _ la _ la la _____ la ___

_ la la la la la _ la _ la la! _____ Wenn Sie

268

Poor wand'ring one
from
THE PIRATES OF PENZANCE

Arthur Sullivan

Tempo di Valse

MABEL:

Poor wan-d'ring one,_____ Though thou hast

sure-ly strayed, _ Take heart of grace, Thy steps re-trace, Poor

rall.   *a tempo*

wan-d'ring one._____ Poor wan-d'ring one,_____ If such poor

rall.   *a tempo*

love _ as mine _   can help thee find   True peace of mind,   Why take _ it,

it ___ is thine!

Take   heart,

fair days will   shine; _ Take a - ny heart,   take mine!

Take heart, fair days will shine; Take a - ny heart, take mine! Ah _____ Ah _____ Ah _____ Ah _____

274

275

Les oiseaux dans la charmille
(Doll Song)
from
LES CONTES D'HOFFMANN

Jacques Offenbach

Moderato

OLYMPIA:

1. Les oi - seaux dans la char -

mil - le, dans les

cieux l'a - stre du jour,

Voi -

*Traditionally, in the fermata, after Olympia's voice weakens, descends, and then stops,
  she is mechanically wound up again.

pi - re tour à tour,

é - meut son cœur, qui fris -

son - ne, é - meut son cœur, qui fris - son - ne d'a-

mour! Ah!

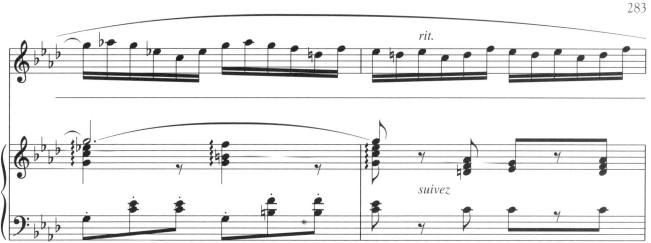

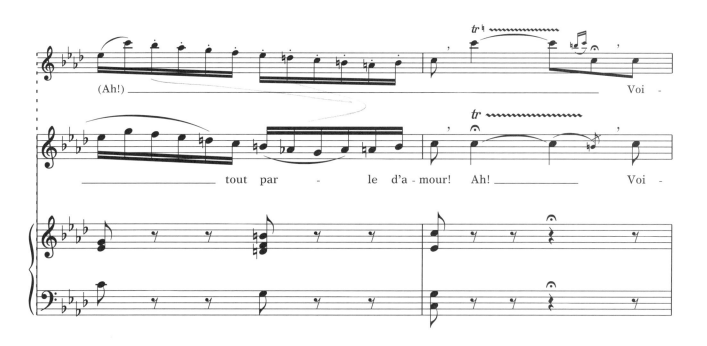

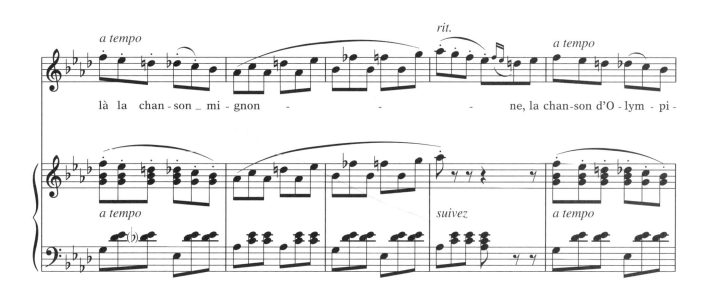

Ah! Où va la jeune indoue

(Bell Song)
from
LAKMÉ

Léo Delibes

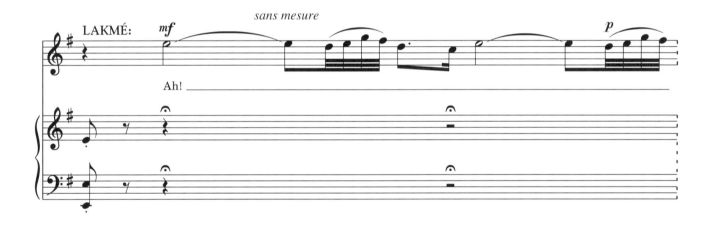

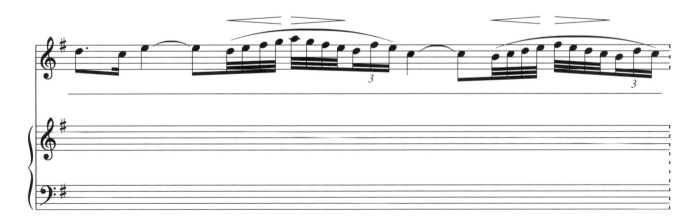

289

Andante *(presque en récitatif)*

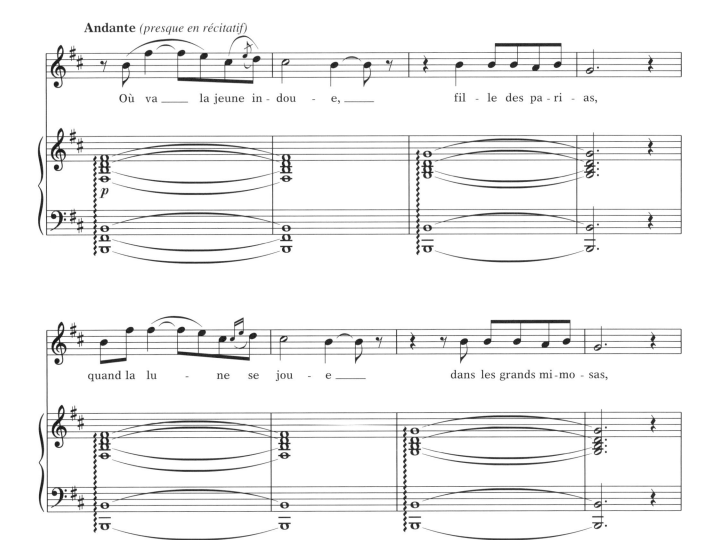

Où va la jeune in - dou - e, fil - le des pa - ri - as,

quand la lu - ne se jou - e dans les grands mi -mo - sas,

290

le long des lau-riers ro - ses,

rê-vant de dou-ces cho - ses,

molto rall.

ah! el - le pas-se sans bruit et ri-ant à la

suivez

Plus lent *rall.*

nuit, à la nuit!

[ah]

suivez

Allegro moderato

Là - bas dans la fo - rêt plus

[Allegro Moderato]

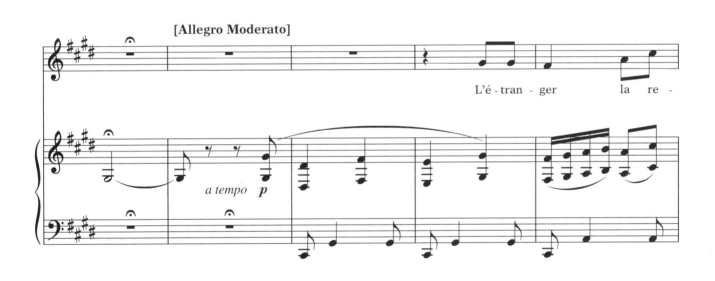

L'é - tran - ger la re -

gar - de; _____ el - le reste é - blou - i - e.

296

guet - te où tin - te la clo - chet - te, où tin - te la clo -

rall. **Plus animé**

chet - te des char - meurs.

p

pp

Ah!

Ah!

300

Otvet' mne, zorkoe svetilo
(Hymn to the Sun)
from
ZOLOTOJ PETUSHOK (The Golden Cockerel)

Nikolai Rimsky-Korsakov

304

сон? _____ Всё так же ль до - рог гость слу -
son? _____ Vsë tak zhe l' do - rog gost' slu -

чай - ный? Е - му го - то - вы и _____ да -
chaj - nyj? E - mu go - to - vy i _____ da -

ры, _____ И скром - ный пир, _____
ry _____ I skrom - nyj pir, _____

и взгляд по - тай - - - -
i vzgljad po - taj - - - -

Großmächtige Prinzessin...
Noch glaub' ich dem einen ganz mich gehörend

from
ARIADNE AUF NAXOS

Richard Strauss

Je-doch, sind wir nicht Frau-en un-ter uns, und schlägt denn nicht in

je - der Brust ein un - be-greif-lich, ein un - be-greif-lich

Herz? Von uns - rer Schwach - heit

spre - chen, sie uns sel - ber ein - ge-stehn,

311

auf Ih-rer eig - nen Gruft.

Sie wol-len kei-ne an -

- de-re Ver -trau - te als die-sen Fels _____ und die-se Wel -

Lebhafter

- len _ ha-ben? Prin-zes-sin, hö-ren Sie mich an— nicht Sie al -

lein, wir al - le ach, wir al - le was ihr Herz er-starrt... wer ist die

Men-schen, ich, ich sel-ber, ich ha-be ih-rer meh-

-re-re be-wohnt und ha-be nicht ge-lernt,

ritard. *accel.*

die Män - ner zu ver-flu-chen. Treu-los sie sinds! Un -

ritard. *accel.*

- ge-heu-er, oh-ne Gren - zen!

tö - rend schon ___ ei - ner nie ge -

ko - ste-ten Frei - heit, schon ei - ner neu - en ver -

p *dolcissimo*

stoh - le-nen Lie - be schwei - fen-des, fre-ches Ge -

cresc.

füh - le sich ein. Noch bin ich wahr und doch ist es ge -

p

318

sein, da mischt sich im Her - zen lei - se be - tö - rend

schon ei - ner neu - en ver - stoh - le - nen Lie - be...

(plötzlich abbrechend)

Allegro scherzando

So war _____ es mit Pa - gliaz - zo und Mez - ze -

RONDO
Allegro ♩ = 54

Als ein Gott kam Je - der ge - gan - gen und sein

Schritt schon mach - te mich stumm,

küß - te er mir Stirn und Wan - gen, war ich von dem Gott __ ge -

fan - gen und ge - wan - delt __ um __ und um.

Als ein Gott kam Je - der ge - gan - gen, Je - der __ wan - - - - del - te __ mich um, küß - te er mir Mund und Wan - gen, hin - ge - ge -

ben, Ah!

Hello! Oh, Margaret, it's you

from
THE TELEPHONE

Gian Carlo Menotti

Jean? You must tell them that I send them my love. And how is
Ur - su - la, and how is Nat - a - lie, and how is Ro - sa - lie? I hope she's got-ten
o - ver her cold. And how is your moth - er, and how is your fa - ther,
and how is dear lit - tle gran - ny? Ha!

Allegro con brio
(nodding)
f brillante
8va

336

Vocalise
from
THE TEMPEST

Lee Hoiby